THE LIFE AND TIMES OF THE
STEAM PACKET

JOHN SHEPHERD

FERRY *Publications*

Overleaf:- The *Ben-my-Chree* [4] towards the end of her career. *(W.S. Basnett)*

Contents Page: Unloading the *Peveril* [4] *(IOMSPCo)*

Acknowledgements

The publishers would like to express their grateful thanks to the following people who have generously contributed towards making this book a reality.

To Malcolm McRonald for both helping to check the proofs and for supplying photographs, and to Stan Basnett, Raymond Brandreth, John Clarkson, Andrew Jones, Keith Lewis and Graham Langmuir for kindly putting their excellent photographic collections at our disposal. Thanks are also due to Miss Vanna Skelley of the University of Glasgow Archives, Phil Eastwood of the Cammell Laird Archive, Martin Crowther of the Imperial War Museum and to Brian Whitehead of the Manx Museum.

Within the Steam Packet, the following gentlemen are warmly thanked for their assistance and encouragement throughout: Dennis Duggan, Mike Casey, John Humphrey, Captain Vernon Kinley, Captain Peter Corrin, Richard Kirkman and Managing Director David Dixon.

Finally, thanks are due to Pat Somner for all her work in transferring the type-written manuscript onto computer disc.

Bibliography

Historical Account of the Isle of Man Steam Packet Company - A.W. Moore, 1904.
How the Manx fleet helped in the Great War - C.J. Blackburn, 1923.
The Centenary of the Isle of Man Steam Packet Company, 1930.
Island Lifeline - Connery Chappell, 1980.
Ships of the Isle of Man Steam Packet Company - Fred Henry, 1962.
Eight Decades of Heysham-Douglas - A.M. Goodwyn, 1985.
King Orry [5]-From Saint to Sovereign - Miles Cowsill & John Hendy, 1992.*
Steam Packet Memories - John Shepherd, 1993.*
A Manx Enterprise - John Hendy, 1985.
The Life and Times of the King Orry [4] - John Shepherd, 1989.
Troopships to Calais - Derek Spiers, 1988.
*British Ferry Scene**
Ships Monthly
Sea Breezes
Cruising Monthly
Manx Transport Review
The Isle of Man Examiner, 1959-94
Annual Reports & Accounts of the Company, 1976-93

* published by Ferry Publications

© 1994 Ferry Publications
12 Millfields Close, Pentlepoir, Kilgetty, Pembrokeshire, SA68 0SA.
Tel: (01834) 813991 Fax: (01834) 811895

ISBN: 1 871947 25 1 (Hardback)
ISBN: 1 871947 27 8 (Softback)

Editor: John Hendy
Design: Miles Cowsill & Ian Smith

Contents

FOREWORD

David Dixon

The Isle of Man Steam Packet is, we believe, the oldest passenger shipping company in the world still trading under its original name. We were incorporated in 1830 and ever since our objective in life has been to provide a reliable and efficient transport link between the Isle of Man and the adjacent islands of Great Britain and Ireland. The primary role was and remains serving the needs of the island population in bringing supplies in, taking goods out for export, and in enabling them to travel to and from. The other main role has been to bring holiday visitors to the Island, to enable them to enjoy a break from their everyday labours in a delightful place, and thus to provide a stimulus to the local economy during the summer season. For a period from the late 19th Century until the middle of the 20th Century the Isle of Man was the only place overseas which was within the reach of a large part of the population of northern Britain and the east coast of Ireland, in the short time they had free to take holidays and with a modest budget. Today greater prosperity allows their children and grandchildren to travel further afield, and the pleasures of the Island are now enjoyed by a discerning minority, who none-the-less make an important contribution to the Manx economy.

This book records the history of the Company from its early days serving the local people, through the boom years of mass tourism, to the vital role it plays today.

I hope you will enjoy reading of these times, and in particular learning something of how our business is conducted in the 1990s.

David Dixon
MANAGING DIRECTOR.

The *SeaCat Isle of Man* rounds the Calf of Man. *(IOMSPCo/Island Photographic Co.)*

INTRODUCTION

The Steam Packet's final passenger only vessel, the **Manxman** of 1955, alongside at Liverpool. *(IOMSPCo)*

"We believe that an account of so remarkable an undertaking as the Isle of Man Steam Packet Company cannot fail to be of interest, and we have therefore endeavoured to put together some of the information we have gleaned about it from various sources."

So commences the Preface to A.W. Moore's "Historical Account of the Isle of Man Steam Packet Company" published in 1904, and these words are as applicable today as they were ninety years ago.

It is now fourteen years since the last comprehensive history of the Company was published. The timeless magic of steam vanished for ever with the last sailing of the *Manxman* in 1982, and after a very difficult period a sleek and efficient organisation emerged, which is the Steam Packet Company today.

This new historical account has been written in chronological diary format. All previous books have had separate chapters describing the fleet, war service, opposition companies and so on. This has meant searching from one chapter to another to find out what happened in a particular year, whereas in this new book all the events of any one year have been recorded together.

I recognise that there is an imbalance in the text with much space being given over to the period from 1945. Surprisingly little research has been done into the years between the wars. Much material from this period, such as old 'Sailing Arrangements' sheets, was destroyed when the Company moved out of the old Imperial Buildings in 1969. A complete analysis of the deck logs of the *King Orry* [4], 1946 – 1975, brought to light much new and previously unrecorded information.

Statistics have been left for the Fleet List at the end of the book and have not been included in the narrative, except where it is necessary to make a point.

The Steam Packet Company has friends and enthusiasts all over the world. I hope that this new book will appeal to them all whether, like myself, they have been sailing on the Company's ships and following its fortunes for nearly half a century; or whether this is the first time that they have read the fascinating story of the Isle of Man Steam Packet Company.

John Shepherd
November 1994

5

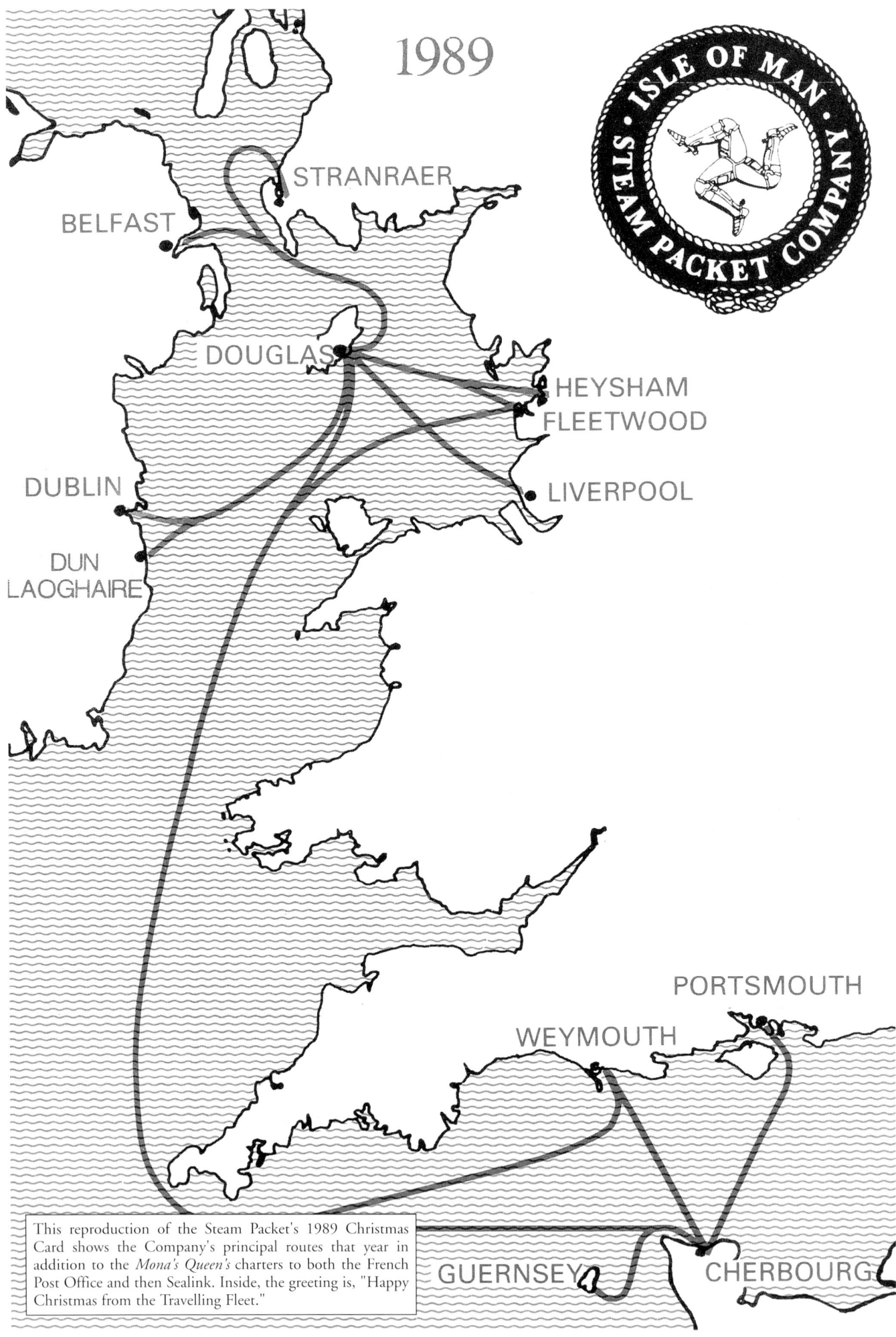

1989

ISLE OF MAN · STEAM PACKET COMPANY

STRANRAER

BELFAST

DOUGLAS

HEYSHAM
FLEETWOOD

DUBLIN

LIVERPOOL

DUN
LAOGHAIRE

PORTSMOUTH

WEYMOUTH

GUERNSEY

CHERBOURG

This reproduction of the Steam Packet's 1989 Christmas Card shows the Company's principal routes that year in addition to the *Mona's Queen's* charters to both the French Post Office and then Sealink. Inside, the greeting is, "Happy Christmas from the Travelling Fleet."

CHAPTER 1
EARLY YEARS

Before 1767 any communication between the Isle of Man and England was by means of vessels sailing at irregular intervals, usually from Whitehaven or Liverpool. However in that year the English Government established a regular 'packet' boat for the conveyance of passengers and mails between Whitehaven and Douglas. The sailings were very much dependent on the vagaries of the weather – in 1813 the mail-packet actually completed fifty-two round voyages; yet in December 1821 only one voyage had been completed in six weeks owing to persistent gales. Given fair weather the Douglas to Whitehaven passage was completed in about six hours, and the fare was 10/6d. (52.5p).

The first mention of a steamer in Manx waters was at the end of June 1815 when the *Henry Bell* anchored in Ramsey Bay. The first steamer to call regularly at Douglas was the *Robert Bruce* in 1819, but during the summer only. The 30 ton *Triton* provided the first regular winter service in 1825, sailing once a week between Whitehaven and Douglas.

The first attempt to form a Manx company to operate a steamer service was made in 1826 when Mark Cosnahan, a Manxman living in Liverpool, purchased the new steamer *Victory* and offered shares in her at £50 each. A meeting was held in the British Hotel, Douglas, on 15th November 1826 but the project fell through.

In 1828 the mail service was transferred from Whitehaven to Liverpool, and the St. George Steam Packet Company was awarded the contract. Summer services provided by this company were generally considered adequate, but during the long winter months the St. George company placed its older and slower vessels on the Manx services, and dissatisfaction

about the state of the steamer service came to a head.

A meeting was held in Dixon & Steele's salerooms on 17th December 1829, which was presided over by James Quirk, the High-Bailiff of Douglas. A committee was appointed to ascertain the probable cost of a Steam Packet and the sum of £4,500 was subscribed in the room.

A company was set up and called The Mona's Isle Company. In January 1832 the name was changed to The Isle of Man United Steam Packet Company, and in July of that year to The Isle of Man Steam Packet Company. The 'Limited' was added in 1885.

In 1830 the sum of £7,250 was subscribed for the *Mona's Isle* in 290 shares of £25, and in 1831 there followed a subscription of £4,750 in 190 shares of £25 for the *Mona*.

The Company's first steamer was launched on 30th June 1830 from the yard of John Wood, Glasgow and named *Mona's Isle*. Her engine had been built by Robert Napier, also of Glasgow, and was one of the earliest models of the side lever type. The 'Isle' arrived in Douglas from the Clyde on 14th August and sailed to Menai Bridge the next day with her owners on board.

The *Mona's Isle* inaugurated the Douglas and Liverpool service on 16th August 1830 carrying 15 saloon and 17 steerage passengers. Her rival, the *Sophia Jane* of the St. George Steam Packet Company started at the same time and defeated the 'Isle' by one and a half minutes. However this was the *Sophia Jane's* last, as well as her first, victory. Both companies were charging single fares of 5/- (25p) saloon, and 3/- (15p) steerage, and following a fierce price-cutting war the St George Company reduced its fare to 6d. (2.5p). Competition between the two companies came to an end when the *St. George* was wrecked on Conister Rock in Douglas Bay in an easterly gale on 20th November 1830.

On 11th July 1831 the Postmaster-General awarded the mail contract to the Steam Packet Company. The mails had to be carried twice weekly in summer and once weekly during

The *Mona's Isle* [1] entered service in August 1830. *(Manx Museum)*

the winter for the sum of £1,000 per annum.

After a year of operating the *Mona's Isle*, the Directors of the Steam Packet Company came to the conclusion that she was too large and valuable to risk on the winter service. Accordingly they ordered a small steamer from the same builders and this was launched as the *Mona* and arrived in Douglas in July 1832. She was slightly faster than the 'Isle' and usually crossed between Douglas and Liverpool in seven and a half hours. On one occasion she is reported as crossing

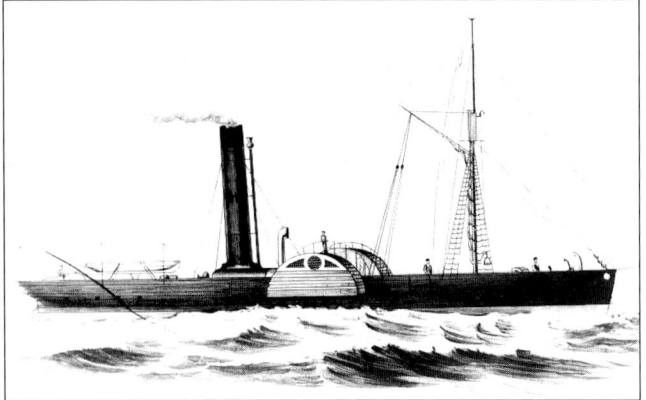

The *Mona* [1] joined the fleet in July 1832 but ended her days as a Mersey tug. *(Manx Museum)*

from Douglas to Whitehaven in four hours and thirty five minutes.

The completion of the *Mona* enabled the Company to expand its services to Whitehaven with occasional Dublin sailings. She commenced service on the winter Douglas – Liverpool service in October 1832 and made the first 'Round the Island' excursion in the following year.

Until 1833 the sailings between Douglas and Liverpool were as follows: twice weekly in March, April, October and November; once weekly in December, January and February, and three times weekly during the rest of the year. The Company used the George's Dock at Liverpool which was on the site of the present Liver Building.

The third wooden paddle steamer in the fleet, the *Queen of the Isle*, was completed in 1834 and arrived in Douglas on 10th September. In the summer of 1834 a daily sailing (except Sundays) operated, leaving Liverpool at 10.00 and Douglas at 08.00.

In 1835 some of the Directors, and shareholders who sympathised with them, seceded from the Steam Packet Company and formed the Isle of Man and Liverpool Steam Navigation Company. This company ordered a 300 ton steamer called the *Monarch* which was built by Steele of Greenock. There was much racing with the *Queen of the Isle* and, just as would happen 145 years later, very bitter feelings arose between the two Manx companies. In 1837 the *Monarch* company collapsed, and there was no more serious competition for fifty years.

1841 – 1850

The final wooden steamer in the fleet, the *King Orry* [1], was also the only vessel to be built in the Isle of Man at John Winram's yard at Douglas. She was launched on 10th February 1842 and the hull was then towed to Napier's works at Glasgow by the *Mona's Isle* for installation of the side lever machinery which gave her a speed of 9.5 knots. Her fastest

passage between Liverpool and Douglas was six hours and twenty minutes.

With the completion of the *King Orry* imminent, the *Mona* was disposed of in 1841 to the Liverpool Steam Tug Company, which had been founded in 1836 as the first organised towing company in Liverpool.

The first iron ship in the Steam Packet fleet was launched on 3rd May 1845 from Robert Napier's Glasgow yard and was named *Ben-my-Chree* [1]. The previous year the Company had sold the *Queen of the Isle* to Robert Napier who fitted her engines into the new 'Ben'. The *Queen of the Isle's* hull was then sold for conversion to a full rigged sailing vessel.

The second iron paddle steamer was launched by Napier on 28th April 1846 and named *Tynwald*. She was nearly double the size of any of her predecessors and was built to cope with the rapidly increasing traffic. The *Tynwald* has the dubious distinction of being the first Steam Packet vessel

The *Tynwald* [1] was an iron-hulled paddle steamer which was built on the Clyde in 1846. *(Manx Museum)*

whose launch was delayed by a strike in the shipbuilding yard.

The Company's pioneer steamer, the *Mona's Isle*, continued to sail throughout the 1840s although the Directors had advertised her for sale from 1837. She was reboiled by Napier in 1845 for £500. The 'Isle' was sold for breaking up in 1851 for the sum of £580.

The Company was experimenting with new routes and in 1842 commenced sailings to Fleetwood. These continued on a spasmodic and intermittent basis over the next 35 years until a regular summer service was established in 1876. Direct Ramsey to Liverpool sailings commenced in 1848, usually once a week.

1851 – 1860

The *Mona's Queen* was launched from the yard of J.& G. Thompson, Govan, on 27th November 1852 and achieved 13.02 knots on trials on 21st February 1853. In September 1853 the 'Queen' made a special trip to Dublin with Steam Packet shareholders as passengers to enable them to see Queen Victoria on her visit to the Irish capital.

A 400 ton steamer called the *Manx Fairy* was built for a local Ramsey company by Laird Brothers of Birkenhead and arrived in Ramsey in August 1853. Racing between the *Manx Fairy* and the Steam Packet's *Mona Queen* began, with both steamers being fairly evenly matched. This 'racing' involved both vessels leaving the same port at the same time and

The **Mona's Queen** entered service in 1853. *(Manx Museum)*

& Company for £4,070.

The Prince's Landing Stage at Liverpool was opened on 1st September 1857 and generated an upsurge in passenger traffic. Passengers could now directly board the Douglas-bound steamer without the delays and inconvenience involved in either being rowed out to a vessel anchored in mid-river, or awaiting the tide to leave the dock system.

In 1858 Robert Napier took the *King Orry* in part payment of new construction. The sum of £5,000 was allowed against the cost of the *Douglas* which was launched at Glasgow on 28th May 1858. The *Douglas* achieved a trials speed of 17.25 knots which reputedly made her the fastest steamship so far built. She was the first two-funnelled vessel in the fleet and reduced the Liverpool and Douglas passage to between four and a half and five hours.

The first repetition of a name occurred on 10th April 1860 when the *Mona's Isle* [2] was launched from the yard of Tod & McGregor, Glasgow. She attained 12 knots on trials on 25th May 1860.

literally racing across the Irish Sea. In August 1857 the *Manx Fairy* ran down and sank the Birkenhead ferry *Fanny*, and her owners had to pay £1,775. In November the *Manx Fairy* was bought by a syndicate of Ramsey businessmen for £7,000 and remained on the station until 1861. Her owners tried to sell her to the Steam Packet Company but they were not interested, and she was sold for £6,000 to Cunard, Wilson & Company.

Now that Ramsey, in the north of the Isle of Man, had established a local Steam Packet Company, Castletown, in the south, was anxious for the same distinction. Laird Brothers of Birkenhead launched the 350 ton *Ellan Vannin* for the Castletown company in June 1854. In smooth conditions the *Ellan Vannin* was faster than the Steam Packet's *Mona's Queen* or the Ramsey Company's *Manx Fairy*. The *Ellan Vannin's* fastest passage between Liverpool and Douglas is recorded as five hours twenty minutes. Whilst the Ramsey and Castletown steamers were built to serve their respective ports, they would put into Douglas on any pretext. In September 1856 the Castletown company was in financial dire straits, and the *Ellan Vannin* ran from Castletown via Douglas to Liverpool at which time the fare was reduced to 1/- (5p). In December 1857 the *Ellan Vannin* was sold to Cunard, Wilson

1861 – 1870

The Liverpool firm of Stewart and Douglas acquired the *Ben-my-Chree* [1] from the Steam Packet in 1862 and adapted her for use as a coaling hulk on the Bonny River in West Africa.

With the outbreak of the American Civil War, the Confederate Government acquired many fast paddle steamers to run the Federal blockade, and the Steam Packet Company sold the *Douglas* [1] for £24,000 to the Confederate Agents, Fraser, Trenholm & Company in 1862. After only four years with the Manx Company, the steamer was renamed *Margaret & Jessie* and was caught and driven ashore by the Federal warship *Rhode Island* off the island of Eleuthera, Bahamas on 1st June 1863. After being refloated and refitted the former Manx steamer continued to run the blockade until her capture by USS *Fulton* off Wilmington. She was taken to New

The **Douglas** [1] was the first two funnelled ship in the fleet and became an American Civil War blockade runner. *(Manx Museum)*

The **Douglas** [2] replaced the earlier vessel of the same name. *(Manx Museum)*

York and fitted out for the Federal Navy as USS *Gettysburg*. With the end of the Civil War the *Gettysburg* (ex *Douglas*) entered the US naval surveying service until finally sold for breaking up at Naples on 8th May 1879.

In the mid 1860s, three generally similar paddle steamers were launched for the Steam Packet Company from the yard of Caird & Company, Greenock. The first of these was the *Snaefell* [1], launched on 22nd June 1863. As a replacement for the *Douglas* [1], a ship of the same name was launched on 11th May 1864; and on 17th March 1866 the *Tynwald* [2] was launched.

The *Tynwald* [1] had been sold in 1866 for £5,000 to Caird & Company in part payment for the new ship of the same name. The new *Tynwald* achieved 14.9 knots on trials on 30th May 1866, and her appearance differed from the two earlier Caird built ships in that both her funnels were situated abaft the paddle boxes.

1871 – 1880

The difficulties of landing and embarking large numbers of passengers at Douglas were overcome in 1871 with the opening on 1st July of the new Victoria Pier. Initially the pier was a very spartan affair providing two deep water berths until

it was extended to its present length in 1885.

The fleet increased to six ships in 1871 when the *King Orry* [2] was launched on 27th March from the yard of R. Duncan & Company, Glasgow. She achieved 14.5 knots on trials on 22nd June 1871.

The *Ben-my-Chree* [2] was launched on 6th May 1875 by the Barrow Shipbuilding Company. The 1,000 gross ton mark was passed for the first time as the new steamer had a gross tonnage of 1,030. She was a slow vessel with a speed of only 14 knots, this being two knots slower than her original contract speed.

In 1875 the *Snaefell* [1] was sold to the Zeeland Steamship Company who changed her name to *Stad Breda* and used her to inaugurate their new service across the southern North Sea from Flushing to Sheerness. On 1st November 1876, King William III of the Netherlands was on board the steamer when he opened the North Sea Canal from Amsterdam to Ijmuiden. The vessel was broken up at Goes in 1883. The *Snaefell* [2] was launched by Miss Caird from the family yard at Greenock on 27th April 1876. On several occasions, the Royal Mersey Yacht Club chartered her as their headquarters ship.

The Prince's Landing Stage at Liverpool was rebuilt in the

Above: The **Tynwald** [2] of 1866 alongside at Douglas. *(G.E. Langmuir collection)*

Left: On board the second **Tynwald** giving a fine idea of the spartan conditions then experienced. Notice the Captain on his raised platform in front of the forward funnel while the helmsman stands below. *(Wotherspoon collection/ G.E. Langmuir)*

early 1870s and was extended in length from the original 305 metres to 629 metres. It was complete and awaiting inauguration by the Duke of Edinburgh when it was totally destroyed by fire on 28th July 1874. For two years Steam Packet sailings were disrupted until a new landing stage came into service in 1876.

A Fleetwood and Douglas service was operated between 1st July and 30th September 1876 in association with the Lancashire & Yorkshire Railway Company. This seasonal service has continued ever since, apart from gaps in the war years, and a break from 1962 until 1971.

The new pier at Llandudno opened in May 1877 and provided a deep water berthing head making it more practical

paddle steamers, and was better suited to the winter service.

In 1879 the daily service (Sundays excepted) was established between Liverpool and Douglas.

1881 – 1890

The last iron ship and the first twin screw steamer in the fleet was the *Fenella* [1] launched on 9th June 1881 by the Barrow Shipbuilding Company. An early mishap on an excursion to Menai Bridge was to strand on the half-tide rock in the Straits. The *Fenella* heeled over to port as the tide ebbed, but refloated successfully.

Despite the success of the early screw steamers, the Steam Packet Company ordered a large paddle steamer from Caird

The second *Ben-my-Chree* failed to meet her contract speed and so was later reboilered, gaining third and fourth funnels. *(Manx Museum)*

to provide sailings to the Welsh resort.

The supremacy of the paddle steamer was first challenged in the Steam Packet fleet by the completion of the *Mona* [2] in 1878. She was a single screw steamer and was launched from Laird Brothers' yard at Birkenhead on 31st May 1878, and attained 12.5 knots on her trials on 15th June of that year. The *Mona* was much more economical to run than the

& Company of Greenock in 1881. She was named *Mona's Isle* [3] at her launch on 16th May 1882, and achieved 18.18 knots on trials on 27th July. This was the first steel vessel in the fleet. Whilst on passage from Glasgow to Douglas in April 1883 she stranded in fog on the beach north of Ramsey. The passengers were landed on to the beach, and the 'Isle' was refloated under her own power later in the day.

The *Snaefell* [2] entered service in 1876. *(Raymond Brandreth collection)*

The *Fenella* was the Company's first twin screw ship. *(IOMSPCo)*

In 1882 the hull of the *Mona's Isle* [2] was considered sound enough to warrant her conversion to a twin screw steamer, and this work was undertaken by Westray, Copeland & Company at Barrow-in-Furness. Her name was changed to *Ellan Vannin* and she became associated with services from Ramsey. On one occasion she attempted to tow the stranded Midland Railway steamer *Donegal* off the beach at the Point of Ayre, the northern-most tip of the Isle of Man.

The Liverpool, Llandudno & North Wales Steamship Company chartered the *Douglas* [2] in 1883. In January 1889 C. W. Kellock & Company auctioned her at Liverpool and she was sold for £1,450 to R. P. Houston for demolition.

When the *Mona* [2] was at anchor in dense fog near the Mersey Bar light vessel on 5th August 1883, the Spanish steamer *Rita* ran into her. The *Mona* sank in half an hour and all her crew and two passengers were picked up by the tug *Conqueror*.

The total number of passengers carried by the Company in 1883 was 286,418.

To replace the sunken *Mona*, the Company ordered a replacement from the Barrow Shipbuilding Company. She was the *Peveril* [1] and was launched on 24th May 1884. Her appearance was very similar to her predecessor, but she was built of steel. Her trials took place on 21st June 1884 when a speed of 14.27 knots was attained.

During 1884 the *Ben-my-Chree* [2] was reboilered and her accommodation was refitted. Two additional funnels were fitted so that she now had two funnels forward of the paddle

The third *Mona's Isle* was built in 1882. *(Raymond Brandreth collection)*

boxes, and two funnels aft. Although she now looked one of the most impressive vessels which the Steam Packet has ever operated, the new boilers did little to increase her slow speed of only 14 knots.

The *Mona's Queen* [2] was launched by the Barrow Shipbuilding Company on 18th April 1885. She achieved 18.5 knots on trials on 7th July and her entry into service increased the fleet total to ten.

The Fairfield Shipbuilding & Engineering Company of Govan had tendered unsuccessfully for the *Mona's Queen* [2]. Fairfield believed in the compound diagonal type of engine for paddle steamers and considered it superior to anything then in use. To prove their point they founded the Isle of Man, Liverpool and Manchester Steamship Company Limited, and built the paddle steamers *Queen Victoria* and *Prince of Wales*. The *Queen Victoria* was launched on 29th March 1887, and the *Prince of Wales* on 14th April 1887. Both ships were faster by half an hour than any Steam Packet vessel on the Liverpool and Douglas route.

Competition was fierce and in 1888 both companies were involved in a price-cutting war. The fares of the Manx Line, as the new company was popularly known, were reduced to 5/- (25p) first class, and 2/6d (12.5p) second class. The wholly uneconomic practice of racing was reintroduced with the rival steamers leaving Liverpool or Douglas at identical times.

On 23rd November 1888 both the Manx Line steamers were sold to the Steam Packet Company and Mr. Barnwell, their Managing Director, joined the Steam Packet Board. As a result of the competition the Steam Packet Company had recorded losses in 1887 and 1888.

With the acquisition of the Manx Line, the *Douglas* [2] and the *Tynwald* [2] were effectively redundant and both were sold at auction in January 1889 and broken up.

The *King Orry* [2] was sent to Barrow in 1888 where she was lengthened by 9.14 metres and her gross tonnage increased to 1104. Her speed increased to 17 knots with the fitting of new compound diagonal engines.

In 1887 the Steam Packet Company purchased the Imperial Hotel at Douglas and, until 1969, established its Head Office there.

Another opposition company was started in 1887. This was the Isle of Man Steam Navigation Company, known as the Lancashire Line, which operated the steamer *Lancashire Witch*. The company lasted until May 1888 when the vessel was sold by order of the mortgagees.

1891 – 1900

The third *Tynwald* was launched from the Fairfield yard at Govan on 11th May 1891. She was a twin-screw steamer, and although she was considerably smaller than the recent paddle steamers, she was, at 937 tons, larger than the preceding screw steamers. The *Tynwald* carried the new Governor of the Isle of Man, Lord Henniker, to Douglas in April 1896.

On the evening of 6th September 1892 the *Mona's Isle* [3] stranded at Scarlett Point, Castletown, when bound from Dublin to Douglas with 400 passengers. She remained fast for two days, finally being refloated by the efforts of the *Tynwald*.

Passenger traffic was on the rapid increase towards the end of the century and 516,359 passengers were carried in 1894. This was an increase of 230,000 on the total of ten years earlier.

A spate of opposition companies was encountered in the 1890s. Nothing as serious as the Manx Line developed, and for the most part they failed to threaten the Steam Packet's strengthening position. The grandly-named Douglas, Llandudno and Liverpool Line was registered in 1894 and announced that three fast steamers were to be built at Barrow. Nothing more was heard of this company.

The Mutual Line of Manx Steamers chartered the former Great Eastern Railway paddle steamer *Lady Tyler* in 1895. She was a slow and outdated vessel, having been built in 1880 for

A magnificent view of the **Mona's Queen** [2] steaming away from Fleetwood. *(G.E. Langmuir collection)*

The *Prince of Wales* (above) and the *Queen Victoria* (right) were acquired from the rival Manx Line in 1888. *(Manx Museum/ Raymond Brandreth collection)*
(Below) The *Mona's Isle* [3] aground on Scarlett Point, Castletown, in September 1892 as the *Tynwald* [3] attempts to pull her clear. *(IOMSPCo)*

The *Tynwald* [3] was built at Govan in 1891. *(Malcolm McRonald collection)*

the overnight Harwich – Rotterdam link, and took six hours for the Liverpool and Douglas passage. The company operated from May until July 1895 and then went into bankruptcy.

In 1897 the steamers *Munster* and *Leinster* were advertised by Messrs H. & C. McIver as commencing on the Liverpool and Douglas service at Easter. The Steam Packet Company stepped in and bought both these steamers and immediately disposed of them for scrap, thus preventing the new service starting.

The Diamond Jubilee year of Queen Victoria saw the launch of the magnificent paddle steamer *Empress Queen* from the Fairfield yard at Govan on 14th March 1897. She achieved 21.75 knots on trials on 8th July and in the following year was averaging 3 hours 5 mins for the Liverpool and Douglas passage.

The *Peveril* [1] sank off Douglas on 17th September 1899 following a collision with the coaster *Monarch*. The *Monarch* was on passage from Workington to Cardiff and although it was clear that both vessels were on a collision bearing, neither altered course. Twelve miles off Douglas at 01.00 the *Monarch* struck the *Peveril* amidships on the starboard side. The *Peveril* sank within forty minutes, her crew and one passenger being transferred to the *Monarch* and later landed at Douglas.

Liverpool & Douglas Steamers was founded by Mr. S.W. Higginbottom, MP in 1899 and placed the *Ireland* on the route. She was a large paddle steamer of 2,000 tons but slow and out of date. This new company then purchased the *Normandy* and *Brittany*, former Newhaven – Dieppe steamers of the London, Brighton & South Coast Railway Company and the *Lily* and the *Violet* from the London & North Western Railway Company. These were all paddle steamers of comparatively small size and slow speed, and Mr. Higginbottom's

company was subsequently operated at a heavy loss. His only successful purchase was to be the *Calais-Douvres* in December 1900 from the Dover – Calais fleet of the South Eastern & Chatham Railway Company's Joint Managing Committee.

The *Empress Queen* was the final paddle steamer to be built for the Company. *(Raymond Brandreth collection)*

THE STEAM PACKET FLEET IN 1900:

Fleet List	Name	Type	Launch	Age	Gross tonnage	Passengers
9	*Ellan Vannin*	TSS	10.4.1860	40	375	299
13	*King Orry* [2]	PS	27.3.1871	29	1,104	1,104
14	*Ben-my-Chree* [2]	PS	6.5.1875	25	1,192	1,030
15	*Snaefell* [2]	PS	27.4.1876	24	849	780
17	*Fenella* [1]	TSS	9.6.1881	19	564	504
18	*Mona's Isle* [3]	PS	16.5.1882	18	1,564	1,561
20	*Mona's Queen* [2]	PS	18.4.1885	15	1,559	1,465
22	*Queen Victoria*	PS	29.3.1887	13	1,657	1,546
21	*Prince of Wales*	PS	14.4.1887	13	1,657	1,546
23	*Tynwald* [3]	TSS	11.5.1891	9	937	904
24	*Empress Queen*	PS	4.3.1897	3	2,140	1,994
					13,598	12,733

PS: Paddle Steamer
TSS: Twin Screw Steamer

Average age of fleet in 1900: 19 years.
8 Paddle Steamers, 3 Twin Srew Steamers, all purpose built for Company.

CHAPTER 2
THE YEARS OF PLENTY 1900 – 1913

The first former railway steamer to be transferred to the Manx registry was the *Dora*, of 1889, which became the *Douglas* [3] in 1901. (*John Shepherd collection*)

At the turn of the century, the Isle of Man Steam Packet Company was operating a fleet of eleven vessels which comprised eight paddle steamers and three twin-screw steamers. The oldest was the *Ellan Vannin* (built as the *Mona's Isle* [2] in 1860), and the newest was the *Empress Queen* of 1897.

Some fairly stiff opposition was being encountered from Liverpool & Douglas steamers and a price-cutting war was in progress. In 1900 a first-class saloon return was available at 4/- (20p).

Until 1901 all the Steam Packet Company's ships had been ordered by and built for the company, with the exception of the *Queen Victoria* and *Prince of Wales*, purchased in 1888. However, a replacement was needed for the *Peveril* [1], lost in 1899, and so on 26th July 1901 the Company purchased the *Dora* from the London & South Western Railway Company. The *Dora* had been built by Napiers of Glasgow in 1889 and had been employed on the Southampton – Channel Islands service. She was a single-screw steamer of 813 tons and was renamed *Douglas* [3] by the Steam Packet and became the first instance of second-hand railway tonnage being bought in.

In June 1901 Lever Brothers of Port Sunlight chartered the paddle steamers *Queen Victoria*, *Mona's Isle* [3] and *Mona's Queen* [2] and took 4,500 of their workers on an excursion from Liverpool to Douglas. Special ferry sailings from New Ferry and Rock Ferry sailed at 05.00, with another special from Woodside leaving at 05.15. The paddlers left Prince's Stage at 06.00 and returned in the late evening.

There was a crop of incidents in the late summer and autumn of 1901. In August the *Ben-my-Chree* [2] collided

with the Powell steamer *West Coast* in the Crosby Channel. A month later in September, the *Fenella* [1] stranded on the Mull of Galloway when she was on passage to Glasgow with 200 passengers. The *Snaefell* [2] was sent to assist and took off the passengers and landed them at Glasgow. The *Fenella* was herself refloated after two days and proceeded to Glasgow for examination.

Whilst on passage from Douglas on 17th September 1901 the Barrow steamer *Duchess of Devonshire* broke a propeller shaft, and the *Tynwald* [3] took over her sailings.

In November 1901 a gale caused the Maryport pilot cutter *Primrose* to be blown off station and to be driven ashore on Langness, the south-eastern extremity of the Isle of Man. The *Fenella* went and rescued the crew.

On 28th June 1902, the Coronation of H.M. King Edward VII was marked by a Review of the Fleet at Spithead. On this occasion, the *Mona's Isle* [3] was chartered to Lunn's for a special cruise from Southampton Docks.

On the death of Mr. Higginbottom in December 1902, Liverpool & Douglas Steamers went into liquidation, and in July 1903 the Steam Packet Company bought the *Calais-*

Douvres for £6,000 and renamed her *Mona* [3] at the same time.

Launched on 6th April 1889, the vessel had been built for the London Chatham & Dover Railway Company by the Fairfield Shipbuilding and Engineering Company of Govan. Her entry into service on 3rd June coincided with the opening of new docks at Calais and the anticipated traffic which the Paris International Exhibition of that year would bring to the Dover – Calais route. A new first class train, which became known as 'The Club Train', was also introduced to link with the *Calais- Douvres* which was at that time the last word in speed and luxury. She became redundant following the amalgamation of her owners with the rival South Eastern Railway in 1899 and was offered for sale. As the third-named *Mona*, she was the final paddle steamer to be added to the Steam Packet's fleet.

The *Empress Queen* was fitted with Marconi 'wireless' in August 1903 and was the first Steam Packet ship to be so equipped.

On 6th November 1903 the *Douglas* [3] collided with and sank the *City of Lisbon* in the Mersey.

The total number of passengers carried by the Steam Packet in 1903 amounted to 711,514. The standard return fare was 10/- (50p).

In 1904 the Isle of Man received its first visit from a steam turbine vessel. The Midland Railway Company's *Londonderry*

Above:- The **Calais-Douvres** on trials in 1889. *(University of Glasgow Archives)*

Below:- As the **Mona** [3], the vessel was the last paddle steamer to be added to the Manx fleet. *(Keith P. Lewis collection)*

Right:- The **Snaefell** [2] ready to be towed to the breakers in 1904. *(S.R. Keig/ John Shepherd collection)*

operated an excursion sailing from the newly opened port of Heysham on Saturday, 13th August. Two months prior to this the railway company had launched the turbine steamer *Manxman* at Barrow on 15th June. With such a name she could only be placed on Isle of Man services.

On the afternoon of Saturday 17th September 1904 the *Queen Victoria* had left Liverpool at 14.30 and was within sight of Douglas when a paddle wheel struck an object and the Master stopped the ship, deciding that it would not be safe to proceed. The *Snaefell* [2] was sent to assist, and the *Queen Victoria's* passengers were transferred to her. The disabled ship was towed back to Liverpool for repairs by the tug *Kingfisher*.

On 2nd September 1904 the *King Orry* [2] was on passage from Douglas to Belfast when, off Maughold Head, she collided with the Ramsey fishing smack *Sunshine* which she then towed back into Ramsey.

At the end of the 1904 season the *Snaefell* [2] completed her service with the Steam Packet Company, and the Dutch tug *Ostzee* towed her away to Holland for demolition.

The Midland Railway Company announced that it would provide regular Heysham – Douglas sailings during the 1905 summer season. On 1st June their turbine steamer *Manxman* inaugurated the service; the afternoon crossing from Heysham being scheduled to take just 2 hours 40 minutes.

To counter this opposition service, the Isle of Man Steam Packet Company placed an order with Armstrong, Whitworth & Company Limited of Newcastle-upon-Tyne for a new direct drive turbine steamer which would be guaranteed to steam at least three-quarters of a knot faster than the *Manxman*. This was the Steam Packet Company's first turbine steamer, and the only vessel ever to be built for them on the north-east coast. She was named *Viking* at her launch on 7th March 1905 and ran her trials on 10th June when 23.53 knots was achieved. She could accommodate 1,600 passengers.

The *Viking's* maiden voyage was from Liverpool to Douglas on 26th June 1905 after which she became the

mainstay of the Douglas – Fleetwood service on which she would burn up to 60 tons of coal a day.

In an attempt to 'cream-off' some of the Fleetwood traffic, the Midland Railway Company sent their new and large tug/tender *Wyvern* over to Fleetwood from Heysham each morning. She would berth at the Corporation Wharf ahead of the *Viking* and embark Douglas bound passengers who sailed to Heysham on the *Wyvern* and then transferred to the railway company's steamer for passage to Douglas. In the evenings this process was reversed.

Above:- The last single-hatch steam coaster on the Irish Sea, the Steam Packet's *Conister*, leaving Douglas during December 1964. *(W.S. Basnett)*

Below:- The motor vessel *Ramsey* joined the Steam Packet fleet in 1964 and is seen here at the Company's cargo berth some eight years later. *(Andrew Jones)*

The old 'Ben'

(Top) In June 1965 the *Ben-my-Chree* is seen on the Victoria Pier awaiting her passengers while the *Manxman* is at lay-by on the Battery Pier. *(W.S. Basnett)*

(Middle) Seen in the same month, the 'Ben' slips away from Douglas on an afternoon sailing to Liverpool. *(W.S. Basnett)*

(Bottom) Laid up at Birkenhead at the end of that final 1965 season. *(John Shepherd)*

The *Viking* crossed from Fleetwood to Douglas in 2 hours 22 minutes in May 1907. *(John Shepherd collection)*

On 31st August 1906 the *Ben-my-Chree* [2] arrived at Morecambe to be broken up by T.W. Ward & Company, and the only four funnelled steamer in the Company's fleet passed into history.

The *Viking* was proving herself on the Fleetwood service, and on 25th May 1907 crossed to Douglas in 2 hours 22 minutes; a record which stood until the introduction of SeaCat services on 28th June 1994. Return crossings from Douglas to Fleetwood on 22nd and 24th July were both completed in 2 hours 24 minutes.

In August 1907 the *Empress Queen* developed paddle trouble whilst on passage to Douglas and had to transfer her passengers to the *Queen Victoria* off the Crosby Lightship.

At the Steam Packet Company's Annual General Meeting in 1908 it was claimed by the Chairman, Mr.D. Maitland, that there was not a turbine steamer afloat, big or little, that could pass the *Viking* between Liverpool and Douglas. As built, the forepart of the *Viking's* shelter deck was open, but a windbreak was later constructed. The first-class passengers were accommodated aft, the usual arrangement in the paddle steamers, although they did not appreciate the vibration set up by the triple screws.

The success of the *Viking* led the Company to order a larger turbine steamer from the Barrow yard of Vickers, Sons & Maxim Limited. She was launched on 23rd March 1908 and named *Ben-my- Chree* [3]. Direct drive turbines coupled to triple screws gave a trials speed of 24.26 knots, with 26.64 knots being achieved on one run of the measured mile at Skelmorlie on 8th August 1908. Going astern, she could make 16.6 knots. The 'Ben' had a passenger certificate for 2,549 and carried a crew of 119. She could burn 95 tons of coal in one day's steaming. The 'Ben's' mean average time for her first season's sailings between the Bar Lightship and Douglas Head was an impressive 2 hours 24 minutes.

Early in the 'Ben's' career, alleged racing in the Mersey channels caused a question in Parliament to be put by Mr. Gershom Stewart M.P. to the President of the Board of Trade. In reply, Mr. Winston Churchill said that he would write to the shipowners concerned. The evening arrivals of the 'Ben' and the Liverpool & North Wales excursion steamer, *La*

Marguerite off the Rock Light had obviously been taken too seriously!

The Isle of Man steamer and the Llandudno steamer were scheduled to arrive at Prince's Stage within five minutes of each other, and friendly racing did in fact take place right up until September 1962 when the *St. Tudno* made her last sailing.

In July 1908 the Liverpool Workingmen's Conservative Association chartered the *Empress Queen* and she took 2,000 people, including three Members of Parliament and the Kirkdale Public Brass Band for a day excursion to Douglas.

The *Queen Victoria* suffered a paddle disablement in August 1908 when on passage from Douglas to Liverpool, and had to be towed back to the Island by the *Prince of Wales.* Back at Douglas she anchored in the bay because of a strong easterly blowing, and the *Mona's Queen* [2] took off her 1,300 passengers. The paddle tug *Pathfinder* was in Douglas and towed the *Prince of Wales* to Liverpool for repairs.

On 9th July 1909 the *Ben-my-Chree* [3] made her fastest

The *Ben-my-Chree* [3] of 1908 approaches Liverpool Landing Stage. *(John Shepherd collection)*

recorded passage on the Liverpool and Douglas run. She crossed from the Mersey Bar Lightship to Douglas Head in 2 hours 16 minutes, and the complete passage, berth to berth, was made in 2 hours 57 minutes.

In September 1909 it was suggested to the Steam Packet Company that their two very fast turbine steamers, the *Viking* and the *Ben-my-Chree* [3] should be chartered out and placed on the service across the River Plate between Montevideo and Buenos Aires.

At the end of the 1909 season the *Mona* [3] (ex *Calais-Douvres*) was sold to Thomas W. Ward & Company, of Sheffield, and broken up at Briton Ferry, South Wales.

On 3rd December 1909 the *Ellan Vannin* left Ramsey for Liverpool at 01.13 with 15 passengers, 21 crew, mail and 60 tons of cargo. A severe north-westerly gale blew up whilst she was on passage, and as the steamer approached the Bar Lightship at about 06.45, the gale reached storm force. In what was to become the worst peacetime disaster ever to befall the Company, the *Ellan Vannin* foundered between the Lightship and the Q.1 buoy at about 07.00. She is believed to have been swept by heavy seas and broached to before

Ellan Vannin, was washed ashore on Ainsdale beach, and was later conveyed back to the Isle of Man for interment. The wreck of the ship was dispersed in March 1910. The steamer *Elm* of 1884 was chartered from the Laird Line for three months to replace her.

On 12th February 1910 the *Snaefell* [3] was launched at Birkenhead. She was the first Steam Packet ship to be built by Cammell Laird & Company (the *Mona* [2] was built by Laird Brothers). The new *Snaefell* achieved 19.57 knots on trials and was extensively used on the principal Liverpool to Douglas winter service.

In 1911 the screw steamers outnumbered the paddle steamers for the first time in the ratio 7:6.

In the summer of 1911 the *Mona's Isle* [3] conveyed a large quantity of bullion from Douglas to Liverpool: an armed escort was provided by Royal Marines from the armoured cruiser H.M.S. *Warrior* which was in Douglas at the time.

During that same year, the Company bought the *Tyrconnel* for the cargo service. She had been launched at Paisley on 11th May 1891 for J. Pinkerton of Londonderry, but changed hands in 1901 to Manx Steam Coasters Trading

reaching the Q.1 buoy, sinking by the stern. All aboard were lost. Later the same day, lifebuoys, bags of turnips and a piano were seen floating near the Formby Lightship but it was not until 8th December that the first bodies were washed ashore.

It will be remembered that the *Ellan Vannin* had been built as the *Mona's Isle* [2] in 1860 and was originally a paddle steamer. In 1883 she was converted to a twin screw steamer when the ship came to be associated with sailings from Ramsey. After the tragedy a fund was set up for the dependants of those lost, and the Steam Packet Company donated £1,000.

The subsequent Board of Trade Enquiry into the disaster had no direct evidence available to form an opinion as to the precise cause. In the Enquiry's opinion, the *Ellan Vannin* broached to before reaching the Q.1 buoy and was overwhelmed by the heavy seas and sank by the stern. The Enquiry found that the ship was in good order and there were no criticisms of the Company, Master or crew.

In January 1910 the body of Captain Teare, Master of the

Above:- The **Queen Victoria** is towed back to Douglas by the **Prince of Wales** following a paddle disablement in August 1908. *(S.R. Keig/ John Shepherd collection)*
Below:- The ill-fated **Ellan Vannin** at the Red Pier, Douglas. *(S.R. Keig/ John Shepherd collection)*

Top:- The launch of the *Snaefell* [3] at Birkenhead in February 1910. *(Cammell Laird Archive)*

Above:- The *Snaefell* leaving for trials on 25th July 1910. *(Cammell Laird Archive)*

Left:- The cargo vessel *Tyrconnel* was acquired in May 1911. *(Raymond Brandreth collection)*

Company Limited of Castletown. She retained that port of registry when she was bought by the Steam Packet, together with her black topped yellow funnel.

An organisation styled the Turkish Patriotic Committee came to Britain in 1911 to buy ships of the cross-Channel type, and acquired the similar *Duke of York* and *Duke of Lancaster* from the joint ownership of the Lancashire and Yorkshire, and the London and North Western Railway Companies. Both ships were sent to Cammell Laird at Birkenhead for complete refurbishment which included reboilering. The outbreak of war between Greece and Turkey prevented the Turks from taking delivery, and the two spare former Fleetwood overnight steamers were purchased by the Isle of Man Company.

The *Duke of Lancaster* was renamed *The Ramsey* and was purchased by the Steam Packet on 12th July 1912. She had been launched on 9th May 1895 and was built by The Naval Construction & Armaments Company Limited at Barrow. The definitive article was part of her name in Steam Packet service, but she sailed for the Company for only two seasons.

Above:- The *Peel Castle* was originally the *Duke of York*. (*John Clarkson*)
Below:- Also acquired in 1912 was the former *Duke of Lancaster* which was renamed *The Ramsey*. (*S.R. Keig/ John Shepherd collection*)

The *Tynwald* [3] was for many years the Ardrossan steamer and she is seen leaving the Ayrshire port for Douglas. (*G.E. Langmuir*)

The *Duke of York* was renamed *Peel Castle* and was purchased on 17th July 1912. She had been launched on 28th February 1894 at the Dumbarton yard of William Denny & Bros..

In 1912 the Steam Packet Company inaugurated a new service from Ramsey to Whitehaven. The *Tynwald* [3] was placed on the run, and in July the first passage was completed in 1 hour 40 minutes. The *Tynwald* will be best remembered with the summer seasonal service from Ardrossan which she helped to popularize from its inception in the early 1890s when the direct railway line from Glasgow to the Ayrshire port was opened.

At the end of the 1912 season the Company announced that they had sold the *King Orry* [2] for scrapping at Llannerch-y-Mor on Deeside, and that a new turbine steamer of the same name would take her place in 1913. The old 'Orry' was open for inspection at a small charge as she lay at the demolition berth and for some years afterwards one of the crests from her paddle box was mounted on the wall of the Lletty Hotel, not far from the scrapping berth.

The *King Orry* [3] was launched by Miss Waid on 11th March 1913 at the yard of Cammell, Laird & Company Limited. Miss Waid was somewhat startled at the launching ceremony when the ship began to move down the slipway before she had finished her speech! This was the first geared turbine steamer in the fleet – these had proved to be more economical than direct drive. The *King Orry's* trials took place on 27th June 1913 when a speed of 20.94 knots was achieved. On her way back from her trials, the new steamer called in to Douglas Bay.

When the review of the ships of the merchant service was held on the Mersey in celebration of the opening of the Gladstone Graving Dock by H.M. King George V on 11th July 1913, the *Ben-my-Chree* [3] was in the line, being anchored in the Crosby channel, off Waterloo, along with the Belfast Steamship Company's *Patriotic*.

In September 1913 the new *King Orry* struck the Victoria Pier at Douglas, and the *Peel Castle* had to deputise for her for some days.

In 1913, such was the boom in Manx tourism that the total number of passengers carried by the Steam Packet Company rose to 1,152,048. This represents the vast proportion of visitors to the Isle of Man, but the Midland Railway Company's Heysham – Douglas service, and the Liverpool & North Wales Steamship Company's Llandudno – Douglas service would increase the total.

CHAPTER 3
THE GREAT WAR
1914 -1918

1914

The Great War of 1914 – 1918 began on 4th August in what should have been the peak of the summer seasonal traffic. Passenger arrivals over the first weekend in August fell away drastically, and at a special meeting of the Steam Packet Directors on 10th August it was decided to lay up the *Ben-my-Chree* [3], *Viking* and *Empress Queen* with immediate effect.

By the end of October the *King Orry, Peel Castle, The Ramsey* and the *Snaefell* had all been requisitioned by the Admiralty which had also asked for plans of all five of the Company's paddle steamers. From fifteen vessels at the outbreak of the war, the Steam Packet's fleet was reduced to four within a few months. The *Douglas, Tynwald, Fenella* and *Tyrconnel* remained to maintain the wartime services – they were all small screw steamers, each of under 1,000 tons. In September the *Tynwald* carried the first of the German war prisoners to Douglas from Liverpool for internment at the special camp at Knockaloe, near Peel. She retained her red funnels, amid the increasing number of grey, to indicate to German submarine commanders hunting in the Irish Sea that German prisoners of war might be on board.

After the outbreak of war the *Snaefell* [3] became an armed boarding steamer, being fitted out by Cammell Laird at Birkenhead. On 18th December she sailed for work in the south-west approaches in the Plymouth Patrol, but in June 1915 left for the Dardanelles.

The Ramsey was requisitioned by the Admiralty in September and went to Cammell Laird for conversion to an armed boarding steamer and became H.M.S. *Ramsey*. She left Birkenhead for Scapa Flow in November. The *Peel Castle* was similarly converted by Cammell Laird.

In September the new *King Orry* went back to her builders for transformation into an armed boarding steamer. She left Birkenhead on 27th November and sailed north to join the Grand Fleet at Scapa Flow.

The number of passenger arrivals fell to 404,481 in 1914. The standard return fare was 10/6 (52.5p).

The *King Orry* [3] off Cammell Laird's yard in which she was built in 1913. *(Cammell Laird Archive)*

1915

The Steam Packet Company's five paddle steamers and two large turbine steamers were pressed into war service early in 1915.

The *Mona's Isle* [3] was sold to the Admiralty in September and fitted out as a netlayer by Vickers Limited at Barrow. The voyage from Barrow to Devonport had problems as the engineer officers and ratings of the Royal Navy were not familiar with her compound oscillating machinery. Her peace-time Chief Engineer was granted a commission and this solved many difficulties.

The Admiralty also purchased the *Queen Victoria* and converted her to a net layer, on which duty she served in the eastern Mediterranean. The *Prince of Wales* was also purchased and similarly fitted out, and her name was changed to *Prince Edward* to avoid confusion with the battleship. Vickers Limited fitted out the *Empress Queen* as a troopship at Barrow in February following her requisition by the Government. In March she sailed to Southampton and immediately started her cross-Channel trooping duties.

The *Mona's Queen* [2] was fitted out at Douglas by the Steam Packet Company for her new duties as a troop carrier. She sailed principally between Southampton and Le Havre.

So much for the paddle steamers. The turbine steamer *Viking* was requisitioned by the Admiralty on 23rd March 1915 and was fitted out at Barrow as the seaplane carrier *Vindex*. The Admiralty purchased her on 11th October and she was stationed at the Nore and at Harwich.

The *Ben-my-Chree* [3] entered Cammell Laird's wet basin on 2nd January 1915 where conversion to a seaplane carrier was carried out. A hangar was built aft of the second funnel which was to house six seaplanes which would be lifted in and out of the water by a crane. There was a flying-off platform forward, of about 60 feet in length. Work off the Belgian coast preceded her departure for the eastern Mediterranean and the Dardanelles campaign.

On 2nd September the 'Ben' rescued 815 people from the torpedoed liner *Southland* of the Red Star Line in the Aegean Sea.

There was once a popular story that the 'Ben' was loaded with ammunition and sent round the Cape of Good Hope to service warships that were under orders to sink the German light cruiser *Konigsberg* which was sheltering in the River Rufiji in Tanganyika (Tanzania). She is said to have made this long journey, from England to East Africa, at an average speed in excess of 22 knots, including stops for coaling. However, as surviving log fragments have shown, it would have been impossible for her to have made the trip in the time between her North Sea operations and her main Mediterranean war work.

On 7th August 1915 H.M.S. *Ramsey* left Scapa Flow on her final patrol. Next day, when she was in the south-east approach to the Pentland Firth, she challenged a supposedly Russian ship which turned out to be the German minelaying raider, *Meteor*. The *Ramsey* was fired on at short range and sank rapidly with heavy loss of life after a torpedo from the *Meteor* had shattered her stern. Fifty two of the *Ramsey's* crew were killed, and forty six were picked up by the raider.

One day later, on 9th August, the *Meteor* was making for the Belgian port of Zeebrugge when British cruisers gave chase. The *Meteor's* crew and the survivors from H.M.S.

The armed boarding steamer **King Orry** [3]. (*Imperial War Museum*)

The armed boarding steamer **Snaefell** [3]. (*Imperial War Museum*)

The **Queen Victoria** as a net layer at Malta in 1916. (*Imperial War Museum*)

Ramsey transferred to a Danish fishing lugger and the Commander of the *Meteor* scuttled his ship so that she would not fall into the hands of the British. The *Ramsey's* survivors were picked up by H.M.S. *Arethusa* and taken to Harwich.

In January 1915 the *Peel Castle* left Cammell Laird and became part of the Downs Boarding Flotilla, a section of the Dover Patrol; and in June the *Snaefell* escorted the monitor *Raglan* to Gallipoli.

The *King Orry* struck a submerged reef in the Sound of Islay when she was steaming at 19 knots on 9th June 1915. Using the hand steering gear, and with only the port turbines working, she proceeded to Birkenhead for repairs in Cammell Laird's dry dock.

1916

On 7th February 1916 the *Peel Castle* was badly damaged by fire after which she was sent to Chatham to be refitted. Later she was transferred to the Orkneys, where she patrolled

*H.M.S. **King Edward** (the IOMSPCo's **Prince of Wales**) laying nets off Condia (Lemnos) in 1916. (Imperial War Museum)*

north of the Shetlands. She finished the war on the Humber/Tyne patrol.

At Easter the *Tynwald* [3] made trooping trips to Kingstown (Dun Laoghaire) in connection with the suppression of the Irish rebellion.

Whilst inward bound to Southampton from Le Havre at 05.00 on 1st February, the *Empress Queen* stranded on Bembridge Ledge, Isle of Wight. Visibility was only a few metres, with light airs and a smooth sea. She ran aground on a rising tide and the 1,300 troops aboard were taken off by destroyers. It was not expected to be a difficult job to tow her off, but after several attempts had failed, a severe gale blew up and she became a total loss.

During the Battle of Jutland (31st May/1st June), the *King Orry* was cruising off the Norwegian coast in company with the cruiser *Donegal* to intercept any blockade runners. In the autumn of 1916 her name was changed to *Viking Orry* for a period.

After the Battle of Jutland, the *King Orry* was used for target towing for gunnery practice and as such, she was able to tow the largest targets at more than 12 knots. At one point

she suffered severe heavy weather damage and was sent to Liverpool for repairs. It is reported that the shore battery at Fort Perch Rock, New Brighton, put warning shots across her bows when she failed to respond to signals.

Towards the end of 1916 the *Ben-my-Chree* sailed through the Suez Canal to the Red Sea for a spell of service, before returning to the Mediterranean.

1917

On 11th January 1917 the *Ben-my-Chree* was anchored in a supposedly safe bay off the island of Castellorizo (off the south-west Mediterranean coast of Turkey). However, the surrounding hills were occupied by Turks who opened fire, setting fire to petrol, and holing the ship which sank in shallow water. The 'Ben' was abandoned after half an hour, and her crew of 250 were able to get safely ashore, with only four wounded. The Master and the Chief Engineer later returned to the 'Ben' and saved the ship's cat and two dogs.

On 6th February 1917 the *Mona's Queen* [2] left Southampton under the command of Captain Cain with 1,000 troops on board, bound for Le Havre. Some twenty

*The loss of the seaplane carrier **Ben-my-Chree** [3] off Castellorizo in January 1917. (Imperial War Museum)*

miles from the French coast a German U-Boat surfaced almost dead ahead. The 'Queen' kept on course, despite a torpedo being fired at her, and the U-Boat's conning tower was struck by her port paddle-box, the steel paddle floats inflicting severe damage. Despite diving immediately the U-Boat (UC.26) was not fatally wounded and arrived at Ostend two days later for repairs and overhaul. UC.26 was finally sunk in the Thames estuary by the Royal Navy on 30th April 1917.

The *Mona's Queen* was disabled by the incident, but managed to steam slowly into Le Havre. After discharging her troops she steamed back to Southampton for repairs at Harland & Wolff, and resumed her trooping duties on 17th March.

In April 1917 the liner *New York* was torpedoed north of the Mersey Bar. The *Tynwald* [3] went to her assistance and took off a number of passengers, including Admiral Sims of the U.S.Navy

The *Snaefell* [3] was converted for troop carrying at Genoa in July and August of 1917.

1918

The *Vindex* (ex *Viking*) was transferred to the eastern Mediterranean in 1918, remaining there until the end of the war. She returned to Plymouth in March 1919 and a month later the Steam Packet Company bought her back from the Admiralty.

At the end of March 1918 the *Tynwald* assisted the White Star Liner *Celtic* which had been torpedoed off the Calf of Man with the loss of six lives. She had been kept afloat by the efforts of her crew and was anchored off Peel. The *Tynwald* took divers and salvage equipment from Liverpool to Peel so that the *Celtic* could be patched up sufficiently to enable her to reach her builders' yard at Belfast.

The *Snaefell* [3] was trooping in the Mediterranean from Genoa, Naples, Salonica, Crete and Cyprus. On arrival at Alexandria in April 1918 she underwent a major refit at the conclusion of which a serious fire broke out on 4th May. Consequently the *Snaefell* was ordered home, but sadly she did not make it as a German submarine torpedoed her when three days out from Alexandria on 5th June.

The *King Orry* [3] had the distinction of following the light cruiser H.M.S. *Cardiff* (Rear-Admiral Sir Alexander Sinclair) and 14 German capital ships at the surrender of the German High Seas Fleet, 40 miles east of the Island of May, at the entrance to the Firth of Forth, on 21st November 1918.

In December 1918, the Steam Packet Company's fleet consisted of the *Fenella* [1], *Tynwald* [3] and *Douglas* [3] available for service, and the *Mona's Queen* [2], *Peel Castle* and *King Orry* [3] under requisition, in addition to the cargo steamer *Tyrconnel*. The two principal passenger carriers the *Ben-my-Chree* [3] and the *Empress Queen* had been lost, as had the *Snaefell* [3] and *The Ramsey*. The *Prince of Wales* and the *Queen Victoria* were not worth reconditioning, nor was the *Mona's Isle* [3]. The *Viking* was purchased back from the Admiralty.

The *La Marguerite* was chartered from the Liverpool & North Wales Steamship Co. from June - September 1919. (*John Shepherd collection*)

CHAPTER 4
THE INTER-WAR YEARS 1919 – 1939

1919

An unusual and important problem faced the Steam Packet Company at the end of the war. The fleet of steamers was dispersed and could only be brought back to pre-war standards at considerable cost. In February 1919 the Company had a capital of £200,000 in £1 shares and had more than £700,000 in investments, plus a fleet which had been written down to a book value of under £70,000. The Company had received more than £500,000 from chartering fees, compensation payments for the loss of steamers, and awards from underwriters.

At the Company's Annual General Meeting some of the directors argued that it would be perfectly possible to wind up the Company if the shareholders so wished, and £5 could be paid out for every £1 of the issued capital. A group of shareholders did in fact propose that the directors should either offer to sell the Company to the Manx Government, or dispose of it as a going concern. The Chairman led a counter attack and proposed that the Company should carry on, this proposal being approved.

A further proposal, that the capital should be increased by a bonus offer of two shares for one, bringing the authorized capital to £600,000, carried the day.

The fleet in 1919 had a total passenger capacity of less than 10,000: in 1914 this figure was in excess of 20,000. Yet with the return of the holiday trade in 1919, incoming passenger arrivals were 343,332.

In 1919 the *Mona's Isle* [3] was offered at auction by Kellock & Company on behalf of the Admiralty, but no bids were forthcoming. T. W. Ward & Company of Sheffield therefore bought her for demolition at Morecambe on 1st

The *Mona* [4] was originally Laird Line's *Hazel* and was acquired in 1919. *(John Clarkson)*

September 1919.

The Steam Packet Company purchased the *Hazel* from the Laird Line on 9th January 1919. She had been launched from the Fairfield yard on 13th April 1907 for the Ardrossan – Portrush service which was suspended in 1914 and not restarted after the war. The *Hazel* retained her name in Steam Packet service until 21st May when she was renamed *Mona* [4].

The *Mona's Queen* [2] was refitted by Cammell Laird in April 1919, and was available for the summer season. The *King Orry* [3] had a period of trooping between Southampton and French ports, but returned to Cammell Laird early in 1919 for complete reconditioning and was back on Steam Packet service in July. The *Peel Castle* sailed as a troopship until May 1919, after which she was returned to the Company.

In order to boost the passenger capacity of the fleet for the summer season the Company chartered the elderly paddle steamer *La Marguerite* from the Liverpool & North Wales Steamship Company from 28th June until 16th September. With her passenger certificate for 2,077 she was extensively used for the period of the charter.

After the war the appearance and general condition of the *Manxman* were such that her owners, the Midland Railway Company, refused to repurchase her from the Admiralty.

1920

The paddle steamers *Queen Victoria* and *Prince of Wales* were both sold for scrapping in 1920 as refitting to Steam Packet standards would have been too costly. The *Queen Victoria* was sold for £5,450 and the *Prince of Wales* was bought by T.C. Pass for £5,600 for demolition at Scheveningen, Holland. It is interesting to note that another Fairfield built paddle steamer, the *St. Tudno* [2] followed the *Prince of Wales* into the demolition berth.

The Steam Packet Company purchased the Midland Railway Company's *Manxman* from the Admiralty and sent her to Barrow for a complete refit in February 1920. The *Manxman* had been bought by the Admiralty in 1915 and converted to a seaplane carrier. Vickers completed work on her in July 1920, and the Company placed her on the main Liverpool and Douglas route in an attempt to replace the *Ben-my-Chree* [3].

The work of refitting the *Viking* was completed by Cammell Laird at Birkenhead in early June and on 25th of that month she was back on the Fleetwood and Douglas service.

On 22nd March 1920 the Steam Packet Company bought the *Viper* from G.& J. Burns & Company of Glasgow. She had been launched from the Fairfield yard on 10th March 1906 by Lady Inverclyde for the Ardrossan to Belfast daylight service. The *Viper* was a direct drive triple screw turbine steamer and achieved 22.09 knots on trials on 1st May 1906. During 1919 she did in fact return to her designed route. After some months of sailing for the Steam Packet with her

Purchased from the Admiralty in 1920 was the *Manxman* [1] which is seen arriving at Douglas. *(John Clarkson)*

original name, she was renamed *Snaefell* [4] on 22nd July 1920.

The third purchase of 1920 was the former South Eastern & Chatham Railway steamer *Onward*, which was launched from Denny's Dumbarton yard on 11th March 1905 and had entered service with a special sailing from Dover to Calais the 4th May with H.M. King Edward VII on board. When serving as a troopship and lying at Folkestone on 24th September 1918, the *Onward* caught fire and was scuttled in order to save the pier. Her superstructure was cut-away and five steam locomotives were used to haul her upright but she did not sail again on trooping service. The Steam Packet Company purchased her when she was lying in Limehouse Docks on the Thames, and she left Union Dock for Liverpool on 15th May 1920. The *Onward* retained her name on Steam Packet services until 27th August 1920, when it was changed to *Mona's Isle* [4].

The final purchase of 1920 was the coaster *Ardnagrena*, built in 1908 by George Brown & Company of Greenock for J. Waterson, Whitehead, Antrim; and acquired by the Steam Packet Company from Humber Steam Coasters as the *Cushag*. She was a small cargo-only vessel with machinery aft, small enough to enter Peel, Port St.Mary, Castletown and Laxey.

In 1920, the first reasonably normal year after the war, the number of passengers carried by the Steam Packet Company was 1,094,220.

The Heysham to Douglas service was restarted in the early summer of 1920 by the Midland Railway Company using their *Duchess of Devonshire* and the *City of Belfast*.

The salvage steamer *Valette* raised the wreck of the *Ben-my-Chree* [3] at Castellorizo in 1920 and it was towed to Piraeus. Following examination, repairs were not considered possible.

The Company's fleet in 1920 was a rather motley collection of thirteen vessels. There was no 'crack' ship. Only five had been built for the Company; the remaining eight having been brought in second-hand. Just one paddle steamer remained – the *Mona's Queen* [2] of 1885 and it was an elderly fleet with an average age of 22 years. The newest steamer was the *King Orry* [3] of 1913, and the oldest was the *Fenella* [1] of 1881. This state of affairs was set to continue for almost a

The *Snaefell* [4] was originally Burns & Co's *Viper* of the Ardrossan - Belfast daylight service. *(John Clarkson)*

decade until the Company's new building programme recommenced with the *Ben-my- Chree* [4] of 1927.

1921 – 1927

In 1921 the *Manxman's* boilers were adapted for burning oil fuel which enabled her to keep sailing through the coal strike of 1926. She was the first Steam Packet ship to use oil fuel.

On 19th August 1921 the *King Orry* [3] ran aground in fog on a falling tide near the Rock Lighthouse, New Brighton, as she was approaching Liverpool with almost a full complement of passengers on board. She refloated, undamaged, on the next flood tide.

In 1921 the standard return fare was £1-2-6d (112.5p).

The *Mona* [4] brought an excursion from Preston to Douglas on Whit Monday, 1922; a sailing that was not repeated for some nearly 50 years.

In 1923 the *Fenella* [1] collided in the Sloyne, off Cammell Laird's yard, with the liner *Clan Cumming*. To prevent her sinking, the *Fenella* was beached at Tranmere.

On 16th August 1923 the *Douglas* [3] was leaving Brunswick Lock, Liverpool when the flood tide swept her across the bow of the steamer *Artemesia* (H.M. Thomson & Company). The *Douglas* was struck amidships on the port side, but fortunately the *Artemesia's* officers had the presence of mind to keep their engines going ahead, thus keeping the

The *Mona's Isle* [4] was also acquired in 1920 and was built as the *Onward* in 1905. *(John Shepherd collection)*

A fourth purchase in 1920 was the cargo steamer *Cushag* which was small enough to enter the harbours at Peel, Port St Mary, Laxey and Castletown. *(Raymond Brandreth collection)*

The 'first' Lady

Top:- Every inch a 'Lady' - the magnificent *Lady of Mann* [1] arrives at Douglas in August 1968. *(W.S. Basnett)*

Below:- Leaving Llandudno on the annual Tynwald Day excursion in July 1970. *(W.S. Basnett)*

The *King Orry* [4]

Top:- Arriving at Llandudno in June 1965 with the *Mona's Isle* in the background on a charter sailing from Barrow. *(Malcolm McRonald)*

Middle: Aground near Glasson Dock in January 1976. *(Malcolm McRonald)*

Bottom:- At her final resting place on the River Medway in Kent during March 1978. Notice that the funnel has weathered to a primrose yellow. *(Andrew Jones)*

THE STEAM PACKET FLEET IN 1920:

Fleet List	Name	Type	Launch	Age	Gross Tonnage	Passengers	Remarks
17	*Fenella* [1]	TSS	9.6.1881	39	564	504	
20	*Mona's Queen* [2]	PS	18.4.1885	35	1,559	1,465	
23	*Tynwald* [3]	TSS	11.5.1891	29	937	904	
25	*Douglas* [3]	SSS	2.3.1889	31	774	506	Built as *Dora*, acq 26.7.1901
27	*Viking*	TrS.DD.T	7.3.1905	15	1,957	1,600	
30	*Tyrconnel*	SSS	29.2.1892	28	274		Acquired 6.5.1911
32	*Peel Castle*	TSS	28.2.1894	26	1,474	1,162	Built as *Duke of York* acq 17.7.1912
33	*King Orry* [3]	TSS.GT.	11.3.1913	7	1,877	1,600	
34	*Mona* [4]	TSS	13.4.1907	13	1,219	1,039	Built as *Hazel*, acq 21.5.1919
35	*Manxman* [1]	TrS.DD.T	15.6.1904	16	2,030	2,020	Purchased from Admiralty, March 1920
36	*Mona's Isle* [4]	TrS.DD.T	11.3.1905	15	1,691	1,479	Built as *Onward*, acq May 1920
37	*Snaefell* [4]	TrS.DD.T	10.3.1906	14	1,713	1,700	Built as *Viper*, acq 22.3.1920
38	*Cushag*	SSS	12.8.1908	12	223		Built as *Ardnagrena*, acq May 1920
					16,292	13,979	

(Total: 13 vessels)

PS: Paddle Steamer
SSS: Single Screw Steamer
TSS: Twin Screw Steamer
TrS.DD.T: Triple Screw Steamer, Direct Drive Turbines
TSS.GT: Twin Screw Geared Turbine Steamer
Average Age of Fleet: 22 years Only 1 paddle steamer remaining - *Mona's Queen* [2] 8 steamers bought in 'second-hand', only 5 purpose built steamers.

bow in the *Douglas'* side and keeping her afloat until all the crew and the fifteen passengers had been taken off by the tug *Fighting Cock*. The *Douglas* then sank and salvage proved to be impossible; the wreck was removed some four months later.

The wreck of the *Ben-my-Chree* [3] was towed from Piraeus to Venice in 1923 for demolition.

In November 1923 the Steam Packet Company purchased the *Caesarea* from the Southern Railway Company. The vessel had been launched on 26th May 1910 for the Channel Islands route of the London & South Western Railway Company, and had been built by Cammell Laird. She had struck rocks on 7th July 1923 and was beached outside the harbour at St. Helier, Jersey. After being refloated she was towed to Southampton for survey and it was there that the Steam Packet purchased her. The Company returned her to her builders at Birkenhead for complete refurbishment and she was converted to burn oil fuel. The *Caesarea* was renamed *Manx Maid* [1] and commenced on the

Company's sailings in the summer of 1924.

The Admiralty Court held that the *Douglas* [3] was solely to blame for the collision with the *Artemesia* at a hearing on 5th June 1924. The Steam Packet Company appealed and the appeal was allowed. However, at a final appeal in the House of Lords, the Appeal Court findings were reversed, and it was ruled that responsibility for the collision lay solely with the *Douglas*.

The *King Orry* [3] aground near the Rock Lighthouse at New Brighton in August 1921. *(John Shepherd collection)*

Left and Below:- The former Channel Islands vessel *Caesarea* (seen -left- leaving the Mersey for sea trials in September 1910) became the **Manx Maid** [1] in 1923. *(Cammell Laird Archive/ John Clarkson)*

In June 1924 the *Peel Castle* stranded in fog in Douglas Bay, but was towed off on a rising tide by the *Fenella* [1].

The *Manxman* developed a steering fault in July 1925 at the peak of the season's sailings, and the Company chartered the *Curraghmore* from the London, Midland & Scottish Railway for seven days.

The major strikes of 1926 disrupted the Steam Packet's operations. The coal burning units of the fleet had empty bunkers, and the *Fenella*, *Tyrconnel* and *Cushag* were laid up; freight being carried on the passenger steamers. Passenger arrivals slumped by some 156,000 in 1926. The main Liverpool and Douglas route was maintained by the two oil burners *Manxman* and *Manx Maid*. From 20th May 1926 sailings between Liverpool and Douglas were reduced to a single passage each way daily, apart from an afternoon sailing on Saturdays and Mondays.

The *Peel Castle* acted as tender to the White Star liner *Albertic* in June 1927 and landed 325 passengers at Douglas on a Manx Homecoming. Three years later she repeated her role, and landed 300 passengers from the liner *Doric* which had anchored in Douglas Bay. The *Peel Castle* came to be associated with the direct Ramsey to Liverpool sailings.

The new *Ben-my-Chree* [4] was launched from Cammell Laird & Company on 5th April 1927. Construction had been rapid – the keel had been laid just over four months earlier on

29th November 1926. Early work on the 'Ben' had been held up by the long strikes of 1926 and Cammell Laird were granted extra payments to meet overtime costs, and promised a bonus of £2,000 if they could meet the delivery date of 25th June 1927.

Trials of the new ship took place on the Clyde on 21st June, and after nine runs of the measured mile an average speed of 22.8 knots was achieved. Passenger capacity was for 2,586: the same figure as her gross tonnage. Her maiden voyage was from Liverpool to Douglas on 29th June, and the passage from the Bar Lightship to Douglas Head was made in 2 hours 27 minutes, giving an average speed of 22.4 knots. In a south-westerly gale the return trip was made in 2 hours 33 minutes to the Bar Light.

In July 1927 Cammell Laird reported a loss of £17,000 on building the 'Ben'. The Steam Packet Company paid £192,000, and then agreed to round the figure up to £200,000. The 'Ben' was the Company's first new ship since 1913, and the first to be built for them as an oil burner.

In August 1927 the new *Ben-my-Chree* was in collision with the *Snaefell* when approaching the Victoria Pier, both ships being sufficiently damaged to warrant their return to Birkenhead for repairs.

The **Ben-my-Chree** [4] at anchor in the Mersey in her original condition. *(John Shepherd collection)*

1928

A policy of rationalisation by the London, Midland & Scottish Railway (L.M.S.) shipping services in 1928 led to the Steam Packet taking over the service from Heysham to Douglas which had been inaugurated by the Midland Railway Company some 24 years earlier. The Company was left with a virtual monopoly of the Manx passenger traffic for the next 41 years.

Two ships were purchased from the L.M.S.. The first was the *Duke of Cornwall* which had been built at Barrow by Vickers, Sons & Maxim and launched on 23rd April 1898. She achieved a trials speed of 19.9 knots, although her service speed was 17.5 knots, and was placed on the Fleetwood – Belfast Joint Service of the Lancashire & Yorkshire and London & North-Western Railways.

On purchase by the Steam Packet Company her name was changed to *Rushen Castle*, and the port of registry changed from Fleetwood to Douglas.

The second purchase of 1928 was the former Midland Railway steamer *Antrim*, which was renamed *Ramsey Town*. She had been built by John Brown & Company of Clydebank, and was launched on 30th May 1904. Throughout her career, she remained a coal burner.

The *Ramsey Town* (ex. *Antrim*) is seen arriving at Liverpool. *(John Clarkson)*

A third ship was added to the fleet in March 1928. She was the Southern Railway Company's *Victoria*, originally built for the South Eastern and Chatham Railway Company by William Denny & Bros. of Dumbarton The steamer was launched on 27th February 1907 and completed her maiden voyage from Dover to Calais on 1st May that year. She was in fact a younger sister of the *Mona's Isle* [4], ex *Onward* and on 11th January 1919 had conveyed Prime Minister David Lloyd George and the Imperial Delegation to the Peace Conference. The *Victoria* retained her name throughout her service with the Steam Packet Company, and made the first Steam Packet

Fleet List	Name	Type	Launch	Age	Gross Tonnage	Passengers	Remarks
17	*Fenella* [1]	TSS	9.6.1881	47	564	504	
20	*Mona's Queen* [2]	PS	18.4.1885	43	1,559	1,465	
23	*Tynwald* [3]	TSS	11.5.1891	37	937	904	
27	*Viking*	TrS.DD.T	7.3.1905	23	1,957	1,600	
30	*Tyrconnel*	SSS	29.2.1892	36	274		Acq 6.5.1911
32	*Peel Castle*	TSS	28.2.1894	34	1,474	1,162	Built as *Duke of York*, acq 17.7.1912
33	*King Orry*[3]	TSS.GT	11.3.1913	15	1,877	1,600	
34	*Mona* [4]	TSS	13.4.1907	21	1,219	1,039	Built as *Hazel*, acq 21.5.1919
35	*Manxman* [1]	TrS.DD.T	15.6.1904	24	2,030	2,020	Purchased from Admiralty in 1920
36	*Mona's Isle* [4]	TrS.DD.T	11.3.1905	23	1,691	1,479	Built as *Onward*, acq May 1920
37	*Snaefell* [4]	TrS.DD.T	10.3.1906	22	1,713	1,700	Built as *Viper*, acq 22.3.1920
38	*Cushag*	SSS	12.8.1908	20	223		Built as *Ardnagrena*, acq May 1920
39	*Manx Maid* [1]	TrS.DD.T	26.5.1910	18	1,504	1,474	Built as *Caesarea*, acq 27.11.1923
40	*Ben-my-Chree* [4]	TSS.GT	5.4.1927	1	2,586	2,586	
41	*Victoria*	TrS.DD.T	27.2.1907	21	1,641	1,536	Acquired April 1928
42	*Ramsey Town*	TSS	22.4.1904	24	1,954	1,840	Built as *Antrim*, acq 11.5.1928
43	*Rushen Castle*	TSS	23.4.1898	30	1,724	1,052	Built as *Duke of Cornwall*, acq 11.5.1928
					24,927	21,961	

THE STEAM PACKET FLEET IN 1928:

(Total: 17 vessels)

PS: Paddle Steamer
SSS: Single Screw Steamer
TSS: Twin Screw Steamer
TpS.DD.T: Triple Screw Steamer, Direct Drive Turbines
TSS.GT: Twin Screw Geared Turbine Steamer
Average Age of Fleet: 26 years Last paddle steamer still remains - *Mona's Queen* [2] Only 6 purpose built steamers, 11 vessels brought in 'second-hand'.

The **Rushen Castle** maintained the Company's service during the 2nd World War. *(John Shepherd Collection).*

sailing between Heysham and Douglas on 23rd June 1928.

The Steam Packet Company's fleet in 1928 consisted of 17 steamers. At one end of the scale the new 'crack' steamer *Ben-my-Chree* [4] was just one year old; whilst at the other end of the scale the *Fenella* [1] was still steaming on after 47 years. The total age of the fleet amounted to 440 years, giving an average age of 26 years, four more than in 1920. The last paddle steamer, the *Mona's Queen* [2] of 1885 was still in steam. Of the 17 vessels, just six had been built for the Company; all the others had been brought in second-hand.

1929 – 1939

A specially designed cargo vessel was launched from Cammell Laird's yard on 25th April 1929 and named *Peveril* [2]. She was a single screw ship and attained a speed of 13.1 knots on her trials on 29th May 1929. Prior to 1929, the cargo services had been operated by outdated passenger vessels and the *Tyrconnel* (acquired 1911) and the *Cushag* (acquired 1920).

On 3rd July 1929 the Steam Packet Company placed an order with the newly formed shipbuilding company Vickers Armstrong Limited at Barrow for a new passenger steamer. The keel laid was on 19th October, the framing was completed on 21st December, and the plating was complete

The **Victoria** backing up the Wyre channel at Fleetwood. *(John Clarkson)*

The cargo steamer **Peveril** [2] of 1929 in the Mersey. *(Raymond Brandreth collection)*

on 27th January 1930.

The end of the 1929 summer season turned out to be time for farewells. The Company's last paddle steamer, the *Mona's Queen* [2], made her final passenger sailing from Fleetwood to Douglas on 31st August. In September she was sold for breaking up for £5,920, and sailed to the yard of Smith & Houston, Port Glasgow.

The *Fenella* [1] made her last passenger sailing in September 1929 from Workington before steaming to Cashmore's yard at Newport, Gwent for breaking up.

In 1929 the Company had based the *Tynwald* [3] at

Blackpool to operate cruises and excursions from the North Pier to Morecambe, Douglas and Llandudno. However they were not successful, and at the end of 1930 the old steamer was laid up at Barrow at the end of her Steam Packet service.

The total number of passengers carried by the Company in 1929 was 1,177,799.

The Isle of Man Steam Packet Company celebrated its centenary in 1930 with the launch of the *Lady of Mann* at Barrow on 4th March by Her Grace the Duchess of Atholl. Trials took place on 13th June when a speed of 22.79 knots was attained. On her first arrival at Fleetwood the 'Lady' was

The Company's centenary steamer was the **Lady of Mann** [1] which is seen going astern towards Fleetwood. *(G.E. Langmuir)*

opened for public inspection for a small charge. Her maiden voyage was from Fleetwood to Douglas on 28th June, leaving at 11.18 and arriving at 14.06 (2 hours 48 minutes).

The *Mona* [4] stranded on Conister Rock in Douglas Bay early on 2nd July 1930 but was towed off with the assistance of the coasters *Texa, Staffa* and *Ben Veg*, and the tug *Strongbow*. Following this stranding, the outer face of the Victoria Pier was painted white to make it more distinguishable from the Tower of Refuge on Conister Rock. The *Mona* was used on cargo-only sailings from Coburg Dock, Liverpool, and also on the winter passenger service.

The *Mona* [4] ashore on Conister Rock in July 1930.*(S.R. Keig/ John Shepherd collection)*

In 1930 and 1931 the Company offered Heysham – Fleetwood – Douglas sailings and also excursions from Heysham to Llandudno.

In her first years of service the *Lady of Mann* had a passenger capacity with a Board of Trade Certificate for 2,873.

On 5th March 1931 the Liverpool & North Wales Steamship Company launched the *St. Seiriol* from the Fairfield yard at Govan. She was a smaller version of the 1926 *St. Tudno* and was designed for the North Wales Company's secondary services and to relieve the *St. Tudno* as necessary. One of the *St. Seiriol's* principal duties was to operate the Llandudno – Douglas sailings, and she was a considerable improvement on the previous vessel on the route, the paddle steamer *St. Elvies* of 1896. Whilst the Steam Packet Company occasionally operated sailings to Llandudno, the traffic from the Welsh resort was left to the North Wales Company and

usually amounted to two return sailings a week in the summer season, accounting for some 20,000 excursionists annually.

In the Spring of 1932 the Diocese of Blackburn chartered the *Ben-my-Chree* [4] to take a group to the Eucharistic Conference being held in Dublin. For this reason the 'Ben's' hull was painted white by Vickers Armstrong at a cost of £63. In the event the charter was cancelled as the 'Ben's' sleeping accommodation was thought to be insufficient, but the white hull remained.

The Company bought the cargo vessel *Conister* in January 1932. She had been built by the Goole Shipbuilding Company in 1921 as the *Abington*, and operated by G.T. Gillie and Blair (Cheviot Coasters Limited) of Newcastle-upon-Tyne. The *Conister* was a single hatch coaster, and the last coal fired ship to be added to the fleet.

In June 1932 the Home Office in London complained

The cargo steamer **Conister** was built as the **Abington** in 1921. *(Raymond Brandreth collection)*

Left:- The *Mona's Queen* [3] is launched at Birkenhead in April 1934. *(John Clarkson)*

Below:- The *Mona's Queen* off Cammell Laird's yard. *(IOMSPCo)*

about the defacement of the red ensign by the 'three legs of Mann' picked out in gold on the fly, as flown by the Steam Packet fleet. This constituted an offence under the Merchant Shipping Act of 1894, and there would be a penalty of £500 for each offence. New flags were obtained and the Home Office advised.

The Company disposed of the *Tyrconnel* in 1932 to S.W. Coe & Company, and she was demolished in Danzig in 1934.

The *Victoria* was refitted at Birkenhead in time for the 1933 summer season, her boilers were adapted for burning oil fuel and the cowls were removed from her funnels at the same time. The steamer became associated with the Dublin and Belfast routes.

The *Tynwald* [3] had been lying at Barrow for three years and in 1933 was purchased by Mr. R.A. Colby Cubbin. He intended to convert her into a yacht under the name of *Western Isles* and as such she lay in the King George V Dock at Glasgow.

The 'Ben's' new white hull had been favourably commented on by the travelling public, and the *Lady of Mann* was painted white in time for the 1933 summer season.

The Steam Packet Company returned to Cammell Laird for their next new steamer, and the *Mona's Queen* [3] was launched on 12th April 1934 with a white hull and green boot-topping. In the 'Ben' of 1927, the 'Lady' of 1930 and the new 'Queen', the Company had perhaps the finest short-sea ships in the world, as well as offering a service second-to-none.

Over the years the Company's cargo ships suffered a number of incidents when passing through or leaving the locks at Liverpool, which gave access to the cargo berth in the Coburg Dock. In 1934 the *Peveril* [2] was stationary in the lock when the swingbridge operated prematurely and removed her mainmast! When repairs were being carried out the opportunity was taken to instal a wheelhouse; as built the steamer had an open bridge.

Right through to the 1980s it was traditional for the Company to bring out a third vessel to cover the Easter sailings, and in the '20s and '30s the *Viking* had been used on many occasions. In 1935 the new *Mona's Queen* appeared for the Easter period, after which she returned to Gladstone Dock to await Whitsun.

The *Fenella* [2] was the first of two Barrow-built sisters and entered service in May 1937. *(IOMSPCo)*

The *King Orry* [3] underwent a major refit at Barrow before the 1935 season, when her appearance was altered with the provision of a new and shorter funnel, and glass screening was fitted to the promenade deck.

In March 1936 two vessels were ordered from Vickers Armstrong Limited at Barrow. A double launch took place on 16th December 1936 when Miss J. Thin launched the *Fenella* [2], and Mrs. Walford sponsored the *Tynwald* [4]. The new ships were specifically designed for the winter service, although neither was provided with a bow rudder.

On Monday, 29th June 1936, the *Mona's Isle* [4] was bound for Dublin when she stranded on rocks at Balscadden Bay, Howth Head. She managed to reach Dublin the same day but as she was making water, repairs had to be carried out there. Passengers for Douglas had to sail via Liverpool, leaving Dublin in B&I's *Lady Longford*. The *Mona's Isle's* appearance was later altered with the removal of the cowls from her funnels.

In the autumn of 1936 the *Ramsey Town* was bought by T.W. Ward & Company Limited for breaking up at Preston.

The *Tynwald* [4] entered service in June 1937 and was painted with white bulwarks. *(Keith P. Lewis)*

The Victoria Pier at Douglas during a warm summer's day in the 1930s. *(John Clarkson)*

The Isle of Man Harbour Board installed a Wireless Directional Beacon on the Victoria Pier, Douglas, in October 1936. Receivers were installed on all the Steam Packet's ships and this helped to eliminate incidents such as when the *Mona* stranded on Conister Rock in fog in 1930.

The new *Fenella* [2] ran her trials on 22nd April 1937 when a speed of 21.81 knots was attained. Her maiden voyage was from Liverpool to Douglas on 1st May 1937 and she soon became a popular ship on day excursions from Douglas to Belfast and Dublin. Her horizontal-topped funnel, also carried by her new sister, the *Tynwald* [4], attracted some criticism and both the new ships had cruiser sterns.

The second of the new sisters, the *Tynwald* [4], ran her trials on 5th June 1937, and achieved 21.68 knots. Her maiden voyage was on 18th June 1937. The *Tynwald* had her bulwarks painted white to window level on the shelter deck, and this distinguished her from her sister, whose bulwarks were black. In 1937 the Manx Government grudgingly agreed to allow Sunday excursionists, and the new *Tynwald* inaugurated special Sunday trips from Heysham to Douglas: as such she became the first steamer to land Sunday

excursionists in Douglas.

In 1937, on the occasion of a Manx Homecoming, the *Victoria* acted as tender to the Donaldson liner *Athenia* in Douglas Bay.

The King Edward VIII Pier in Douglas Harbour was commissioned in 1937, and provided two more deep water berths. The new pier was far less exposed to easterly gales than the Victoria Pier.

The new *Tynwald* [4] operated a series of excursions to Ardrossan in 1938 during the period of the Empire Exhibition held in Bellahouston Park, Glasgow. New fuelling arrangements that year resulted in regular switches in service between the Liverpool and Fleetwood steamers to enable bunkering to be carried out at Liverpool.

During the August Bank Holiday weekend of 1938 the *Victoria* was chartered for £450 to the L.M.S. Railway and operated one round trip on the Holyhead – Dun Laoghaire service.

In September 1938, at the time of the Munich crisis, the *Manx Maid* and the *King Orry* were requisitioned for Government service. However the tension eased and the matter was suspended.

In the summer of 1937 and 1938 the Company operated a fleet of 18 steamers, the highest number ever in its history, and a fleet total never to be exceeded. Two more of the older units of the Steam Packet fleet were withdrawn at the end of the 1938 season, and the *Mona* [4] left for breaking up at the yard of E.G. Rees, Llanelli, in December. In February 1939, the *Peel Castle* was sold to Arnott, Young & Company Limited of Dalmuir for scrapping.

The *King Orry* was converted to burn oil fuel in time for the 1939 summer season. As the proverbial war clouds gathered over Europe, the *Ben-my-Chree* was rostered to provide a series of particularly

The *King Orry* [3] in 1939 with a shortened funnel and a glass screen on the shelter deck. *(Raymond Brandreth collection)*

attractive excursion sailings from Liverpool to Douglas, every Sunday from 25th June until 20th August. Three hours were allowed ashore, and a contract ticket for all nine excursions cost just £1-15-0d. (£1.75).

On the outbreak of war on 3rd September 1939, the Company had a fleet of sixteen steamers. The three cargo steamers *Peveril* [2], *Conister* and *Cushag* were retained by the Company, and initially the *Rushen Castle* and the *Victoria* were left to maintain the wartime passenger sailings.

The *King Orry* entered Sandon Dock, Liverpool, along with the North Wales steamer *St. Tudno* for conversion to an Armed Boarding Vessel. She was assigned to the Dover Command with effect from 27th September. The *Manx Maid* and the *Mona's Isle* also became Armed Boarding Vessels.

The remaining eight passenger steamers all became personnel carriers and conveyed part of the British Expeditionary Force to France.

The old *Tynwald* [3] (now the *Western Isles*) was moved from Glasgow to Wallasey Dock, Birkenhead, where she became the accommodation/supply ship H.M.S. *Eastern Isles*.

CHAPTER 5
THE SECOND WORLD WAR 1939 – 1945

The principal event of 1940 was Operation Dynamo, the evacuation of troops from Dunkirk, which lasted from 26th May until 4th June. The total number of troops landed in England from Dunkirk is given as 338,226, and of these 24,669 were brought out on the eight steamers of the Isle of Man Steam Packet Company which took part in the operation..

The 29th May 1940 was perhaps the blackest day in the long and honourable history of the Steam Packet Company. At 05.30 the *Mona's Queen* was approaching Dunkirk and when one mile off the port she detonated a magnetic mine which caused her to break in two and sink. Twenty four of her crew were lost, seventeen of them from the Isle of Man.

Later that same day, the *Fenella* was berthed starboard side to the east mole stone jetty at Dunkirk, astern of the General Steam Navigation's paddle steamer *Crested Eagle* and with the North Wales steamer *St. Seiriol* standing off. She had 650 troops on board when a force of German aircraft bombed the pier at 17.00 with such effect that heavy stone portions crashed into the side of the *Fenella*, and her engine room was flooded, causing her to settle on an even keel. The *Crested Eagle* was destroyed with heavy loss of life, whilst the *St. Seiriol* rendered all possible assistance.

The 29th May also claimed the *King Orry* which was bombed in the approaches to Dunkirk and was severely

Above and Left:-
The six year old **Mona's Queen** [3] sinking by the stern after having broken her back when detonating a mine in the approaches to Dunkirk on 29th May 1940. *(Imperial War Museum)*

damaged. She was ordered to clear the harbour and the approach channel before she sank. Shortly after 02.00 on the morning of 30th May she sank after her engine room flooded.

The Company had lost three of its steamers in just twenty one hours.

The *Mona's Isle* was the first ship to leave Dover when Operation Dynamo started. She brought out a total of 2,634 troops in two round trips. She was badly damaged and her name was erroneously broadcast in the first list of Dunkirk losses.

The *Manxman* made two trips, and actually grounded on Cap Gris Nez, near Calais, but got off safely. On the night of 2nd June, after completing three round trips, the *Ben-my-Chree* was in collision with another vessel soon after leaving Folkestone for Dunkirk, and this finished her involvement in the operation. The *Lady of Mann* took 4,262 men back to Dover on four crossings from Dunkirk. The *Tynwald* is recorded as making a total of four round trips and bringing out 8,953 troops. On 29th May she passed her sister for the last time; on her next trip the *Tynwald* berthed ahead of the *Fenella* which was submerged up to shelter deck level.

A fortnight after Dunkirk, the *Lady of Mann* was assigned to Operation Ariel, the evacuation of troops from Le Havre, Cherbourg and Brest. On one sailing from Le Havre, the 'Lady' had 5,000 troops on board. The *Manxman, Tynwald* and *Manx Maid* were also involved in the operation, and on one trip the *Manx Maid* brought out 3,000 troops from Brest – double her normal complement.

The *Manxman* was the final troop ship to escape from Cherbourg, steaming away to safety as the Germans were entering the port area. Rommel described her as the, 'cheeky two funnel steamer.' She was also the last ship out of St. Malo.

Just before the invasion of the Channel Islands on 1st July 1940 the *Viking* steamed into St. Peter Port, Guernsey, and took 1,800 children to the safety of Weymouth.

The *Manx Maid* and the *Viking* took no part in the Dunkirk evacuation, as they were both undergoing repairs at the time. The *Snaefell* had been returned to the Steam Packet Company at Easter 1940, and was operating the passenger services along with the *Rushen Castle* and the *Victoria*.

From August 1940 until April 1944 the *Lady of Mann* was assigned to troop transport duties, often based at Lerwick in the Shetland Isles . On occasions she tendered the liner *Queen Mary* at the Tail of the Bank in the Firth of Clyde. In the second half of 1940 the *Tynwald* was based at Liverpool from where she made trips to the Clyde anchorage with German prisoners of war for transport to Canada.

Whilst on passage from Douglas to Liverpool on 20th December 1940, the *Victoria* exploded two mines in her wake, but reached port unscathed. When outward bound to Douglas on 27th December, and about eight miles north-west of the Bar Lightship, she detonated another mine which severely disabled her. Fortunately it was flat calm and H.M.Y. *Evadne* stood by and a number of the 200 passengers were taken off by the trawler *Michael Griffiths* and the Bar pilot cutter. The *Victoria* remained afloat and was towed back to the Mersey by the minesweeping trawlers *Doon* and *Hornbeam*.

After this incident the Company's passenger operations were transferred to Fleetwood from 28th December 1940.

There was a popular myth at one time that the *Fenella* was raised when the mess of Dunkirk was being cleared, and that the ship was brought into harbour and eventually towed away. The myth continued that the *Fenella* was repaired, renamed *Reval*, and that the Germans used her as a troopship between Baltic ports and Norway. Research in the German Naval Archives however, shows that the *Fenella* was broken up where she lay.

To conclude the events of 1940, the following is of interest on a lighter note. On Saturday, 27 January, the *Rushen Castle* sailed from Liverpool for Douglas at 10.45. An easterly gale blew up which made Douglas unapproachable, and the Master was sent a message by radio which instructed him to "Go to the east", namely Douglas. The message should have read "Go to the west", or Peel. Captain Bridson duly arrived off Douglas, and was then signalled to proceed to Peel. By the time the *Rushen Castle* had arrived off Peel the gale had backed, and berthing was not possible. Eventually the old steamer did get into Peel – at 10.00 on Tuesday, 30th January after being at sea for 71 hours. The Lieutenant-Governor of the Island at the time – the Earl of Granville – was one of the passengers. His comments are not recorded.

1941

The *Tynwald* was converted to an auxiliary anti-aircraft cruiser and most of her superstructure was removed, leaving virtually only the hull, funnel and machinery. She was commissioned on 1st October 1941, and took up convoy escort work in the Western approaches.

The *Mona's Isle* joined the Rosyth Command after refit becoming the A.A. guardship at Methil in the Firth of Forth but was decommissioned on the Tyne in November 1943 and came under the control of Sea Transport, Newcastle. The following year she steamed to Scapa Flow and then onto the Clyde via Stornoway. On being handed back to the Steam Packet she had circumnavigated the British Isles.

After her mine damage had been repaired the *Victoria* did not return to the Company, but was requisitioned and fitted out as an LSI (Landing Ship Infantry), and then worked on the Firth of Forth as a target vessel.

From 1941 until the beginning of 1944 the *Ben-my-Chree* was a troop transporter, operating between north British ports and Iceland.

In October 1941 the *Manxman* was again purchased by the Admiralty and was commissioned in the Royal Navy as H.M.S. *Caduceus*. She was attached to the Navy RDF training establishment H.M.S. Valkyrie which had been set up in hotels on the Loch Promenade, Douglas. The *Manxman* (H.M.S. *Caduceus*) was fitted out as an RDF (Radar) training ship at Birkenhead, and provided sea training for H.M.S. Valkyrie. Two collisions with the Victoria Pier at Douglas resulted in Company officers being given temporary commissions to handle ships in Douglas harbour, and the Admiralty stated that the ship was far too large to be used in the port of Douglas at all ! She was moved to the Clyde in 1943 and was not decommissioned until 1945 when she took on the role of a troopship.

1942

H.M.S. *Tynwald* took part in the North Africa campaign and was assigned to Operation Torch. She bunkered at Algiers before becoming part of a task force sent to capture an airfield

A.A. Escort Vessel *H.M.S. Tynwald* [4] which was torpedoed and sunk off Bougie, Algeria, in November 1942. She bears little resemblance to the steamer seen on page 39. *(Imperial War Museum)*

at Bougie, 100 miles to the east. After surviving a severe enemy bombing attack, she anchored in Bougie Bay on the night of 11th November 1942. In the early hours of 12th November the Italian submarine *Argo* attacked her with two torpedoes and the *Tynwald* sank with the loss of three officers and seven ratings. This was the Company's fourth and final war loss.

The *Viking* served as a Fleet Air Arm target vessel based at Crail, Fife, during the latter half of 1942. In December the *Manx Maid's* name was changed to H.M.S. *Bruce*. Among her special duties was that of acting as target ship for the aircraft training for the destruction of the German battleship *Tirpitz*. She continued as a Fleet Air Arm target until March 1945.

1943

In the summer of 1943 the *Victoria* (as an LSI) transferred from the Firth of Forth to Southampton where she was employed in training infantry for the invasion of Europe. From 1943 until 1945 the *Viking* was a personnel ship: she was a coal burner and suitable bunkering arrangements always presented problems.

The Steam Packet Company sold the *Cushag* in 1943 to T. Dougal, of Glasgow, who registered her at Stornoway. He disposed of her in 1947 to Bremner & Company of Kirkwall, Orkney, who retained her for a further ten years before selling her to Grangemouth shipbreakers in 1957.

1944

In January 1944 the *Ben-my-Chree* went to North Shields to be fitted out as an LSI, carrying six landing craft. After this conversion she was in the English Channel, working up for

D-Day. On 6th June the 'Ben' was at Omaha Beach as Headquarters ship for the 514th Assault Flotilla.

Like the 'Ben', the *Lady of Mann* had been converted to an LSI and also carried six landing assault craft. The 'Lady' was Headquarters ship for the 512th Assault Flotilla, responsible for landings on Juno Beach area near Courselles.

On D-Day the *Victoria* landed assault forces at Arromanches, and for some days after landed American forces on Utah Beach.

Considerable damage was caused to the *Viking* on 28th June when a V1 flying bomb exploded nearby as she was lying at Rotherhithe on the Thames.

1945

With the impending end of the war in Europe, the *Viking* was derequisitioned in May 1945 and left Tilbury on 17th May, arriving in Barrow on 23rd May. She was overhauled at Barrow and at Birkenhead, and she returned to the Fleetwood service on 18th June, still with her hull grey, but with her Steam Packet funnel colours restored. It will be remembered that the Company's services had been transferred to Fleetwood on 28th December 1940 following the *Victoria's* mining, and there was no Liverpool service until 8th April 1946.

The *Mona's Isle* [4] was returned to the Company in May 1945, re-entering service in July. Her mainmast, removed during war service, was not replaced.

The *Snaefell* [4] completed her sailings for the Company in July 1945 on account of her deteriorating condition, and in October the tug *Thames* towed her from Douglas to Port Glasgow where she lay at Smith & Houston's yard for three

THE STEAM PACKET FLEET IN 1945:

Fleet List	Name	Type	Launch	Age	Gross Tonnage	Passengers	Remarks
27	*Viking*	Tr.S.DD.T	7.3.1905	40	1.957	1,600	
35	*Manxman* [1]	Tr.S.DD.T	15.6.1904	41	2,030	2,020	Purchased from Admiralty 1920
37	*Snaefell* [4]	Tr.S.DD.T	10.3.1906	39	1,713	1,700	Built as *Viper*, acq 22.3.1920
36	*Mona's Isle* [4]	Tr.S.DD.T	11.3.1905	40	1,691	1,479	Built as *Onward*, acq May 1920
39	*Manx Maid* [1]	Tr.S.DD.T	26.5.1910	35	1,504	1,470	Built as *Caesarea*, acq 27.11.1923
40	*Ben-my-Chree* [4]	TSS.GT	5.4.1927	18	2,586	2,586	
41	*Victoria*	Tr.S.DD.T	27.2.1907	38	1,641	1,536	Acquired April 1928
43	*Rushen Castle*	TSS	23.4.1898	47	1,724	1,052	Built as *Duke of Cornwall*, acq 11.5.1928
44	*Peveril* [2]	SSS	25.4.1929	16	798		
45	*Lady of Mann* [1]	TSS.GT	4.3.1930	15	3,104	2,873	
46	*Conister*	SSS	13.9.1921	24	411		Built as Abington, acq 8.1.1932
					19,159	16,316	

(Total: 11 vessels)

SSS: Single Screw Steamer
TSS: Twin Screw Steamer
Tr.S.DD.T: Triple Screw Steamer, Direct Drive Turbines
TSS.GT: Twin Screw Geared Turbine Steamer
Average Age of Fleet: 32 years 4 purpose built steamers, 7 bought in 'second-hand'. In 1945 the *Manxman*, *Ben-my-Chree*, *Lady of Mann* and *Victoria* were still requisitioned by the Admiralty. The *Manx Maid* was laid up at Barrow until 1946.

The *Ben-my-Chree* [4] arriving at Dover's Admiralty Pier on 18th June 1944, transporting the First Release Group of the British Army to England. *(IOMSPCo)*

years before demolition. Her main companionway was installed in the Master Mariners' ship *Wellington,* moored in the Thames.

The *Manx Maid* was returned to the Steam Packet Company on 21st March 1945, at Ardrossan. On 27th May she arrived at Barrow and was laid up until the 1946 summer season.

H.M.S. *Caduceus* was derequisitioned in 1945 and reverted to her original name of *Manxman.* She was refitted for use as a troopship and during 1946 operated from Tilbury to Ostend, Harwich – Hook of Holland and later still from Dover to Calais.

The policy of the post-1918 period in buying in second-hand tonnage was not repeated, and when it became reasonable to expect an Allied victory an order was placed with Cammell Laird for two passenger steamers, and the keel of the first was laid on 1st February 1945. With the coming of peace on 8th May 1945, construction was speeded up, and the ship was launched on 22nd November to become the *King Orry* [4]. The design was a development of the *Fenella* and *Tynwald* and the new ship and her sisters were designed for service throughout the year.

In 1945, prior to the launch of the new *King Orry,* the Company had a fleet of eleven vessels with a total age of 353 years, giving an amazing average age of 32 years. Only four of the fleet had been built to the Company's specifications; the majority of the fleet consisted of the second-hand tonnage purchased in the 1920s. The Company's three newest purpose-built steamers had been war losses: the *Mona's Queen* of 1934, and the 1936 twin-sisters *Tynwald* and *Fenella.* Within a decade the situation would be transformed as the Company embarked on a rapid new building programme.

The war-scarred *Lady of Mann* on her return to Douglas on the completion of her war service on 9th March 1946. *(Raymond Brandreth collection)*

CHAPTER 6
THE POST WAR YEARS 1946 – 1961

The *Lady of Mann* returned to Douglas on 9th March 1946 at the end of her war service and was given a civic reception. After a partial reconditioning by Cammell Laird in Morpeth Dock, she re-entered Steam Packet service on 14th June.

Meanwhile, the *King Orry* [4] ran her trials on 12th April, when a speed of 21.6 knots was achieved. On her way up to the Clyde, the new steamer called in to Douglas on 11th April to collect a party of Company officials who attended the trials. Her first arrival at Douglas is remembered by Captain

The first of the Company's post-war steamers was the *King Orry* [4]. She is seen arriving at Liverpool in April 1951 after having crossed the Mersey from overhaul at Birkenhead. *(Keith P. Lewis)*

The *King Orry* [4]

Top:- The First Class Dining Saloon.

Above:- The First Class Dining Saloon looking aft.

Left:- The First Class Main Lounge.

(Collection of Stewart Bale)

The *King Orry* [4]

Top:- The First Class Ladies' Lounge.

Right:- The Shelter Deck, port side, looking aft.

(Collection of Stewart Bale)

J.E. Ronan, for many years a Master with the Company, and now retired. In April 1946, he was a seaman (boy rating) on the *Mona's Isle* and he writes:

"Probably the most vivid and exciting moment of that time was when the new *King Orry* arrived from Cammell Laird. The lads from the 'Isle' crossed the King Edward Pier to have a look at this new and beautiful ship. We were still in the aftermath of war with its grim austerities, and it was a most wonderful experience to perceive all those modern furnishings and gadgets, the magic of which in later life, when looking over new ships (and there were many) was never quite recaptured."

The *King Orry* was delivered to the Company on 16th April, and her maiden voyage was from Liverpool to Douglas on Maundy Thursday, 18th April, when she left Prince's Stage at 10.57 and arrived at Douglas at 14.35, a passage of 3 hours 38 minutes. (The Company's service had been transferred back to Liverpool from Fleetwood on 8th April.)

Smit's tug *Ganges* on 9th January 1947.

Throughout 1946 the *Victoria* sailed as a unit of the leave service from Dover, and the *Manxman* was running on the repatriation service.

1947

The *Manx Maid* was winter steamer during the notorious weather of January, February and March 1947, running with the *Mona's Queen* until 28th February, and then with the *King Orry*. Despite frequent easterly gales, no use was made of Peel as an alternative port to Douglas: analysis of the logs for the winter sailings shows that the first time that Peel was used as a diversionary port was on 27th January 1954. Conditions at Douglas became very difficult in strong easterlies, necessitating the steamer to seek a safe anchorage, very often in Port Erin Bay, rather than remain overnight in Douglas harbour.

The *Victoria* completed her trooping duties between

The *Victoria* off Calais in August 1946. At this time, she was engaged in trooping. *(Keith P. Lewis)*

The *Ben-my-Chree* [4] arrived in Morpeth Dock, Birkenhead, at 17.30 on 11th May 1946 after derequisitioning. She was in an appalling state, but Cammell Laird had her ready to enter service on Saturday 6th July, carrying a temporary, shortened mainmast. During an extensive overhaul at the end of 1946, the 'Ben's' mainmast was restored to its original height, but her funnel was considerably shortened.

The *Manx Maid* re-entered passenger service at Whitsun 1946 after being laid up at Barrow for a year. Her mainmast, which had been removed in 1939, was not replaced. The *Viking* appeared for the summer season on 21st June.

The new *Mona's Queen* [4] had been launched at Birkenhead on 5th February 1946. She ran her trials on the Clyde on 21st June, and 21.65 knots was reached. Her maiden voyage was from Liverpool to Douglas on 26th June. For a couple of years the black hull paint extended to shelter deck window level and made it possible to distinguish her from the *King Orry*. A similar arrangement had distinguished the 1936 sisters *Fenella* and *Tynwald*. The 'Queen' and the 'Orry' both provided eight very comfortable private cabins, and a system of prior booking of cabins was introduced with their entry into service.

On Saturday, 14th September, the *Rushen Castle* made her final crossing from Fleetwood to Douglas, and in November the Belgian firm of Van Heyghen Freres bought her for demolition. She left Douglas bound for Ghent under tow of

Dover and Calais in February 1947, and returned to Birkenhead on 7th March. Her first passenger sailings back on Steam Packet service took place on 11th June.

Another new steamer was launched from Cammell Laird's yard on 24th March as the *Tynwald* [5]. She ran her trials on the Clyde on 27th July and attained 21.65 knots. Her maiden voyage was from Liverpool to Douglas on 31st July. The *Tynwald* was very similar to both the earlier *King Orry* and the *Mona's Queen*, the main difference being that she had a 'well' for loading cars on both sides, whereas the earlier two ships had such a 'well' on the starboard side only. This meant that when it was necessary to crane vehicles off the 'Orry' or the 'Queen' they had to berth starboard side to the pier. The Company had never been particularly enthusiastic over the carriage of vehicles on its passenger steamers, pointing out that whilst it was perfectly possible to embark or disembark passengers across the decks of other steamers when they were double or even triple berthed, vehicles had to have a pierside berth at which to be loaded or discharged.

The summer season of 1947 started early for the *Lady of Mann* with her first sailings on Friday 2nd May. At the end of the summer the *Mona's Isle* [4] made her final sailing from Liverpool to Douglas on 29th August, after which she was laid up at 'The Tongue' in the inner harbour at Douglas.

Throughout 1947 the *Manxman* was on contract to the British Government and was usually to be found carrying displaced persons between Harwich and the Hook of

Left:- The *Mona's Queen*, of 1946, arriving at Liverpool. *(Raymond Brandreth collection)*

Middle:- The *Tynwald* was the third of the post war steamers. *(IOMSPCo)*

Below:- The *Snaefell* sweeping into Douglas after a lively crossing from Liverpool. She joined the fleet in July 1948. *(W.S. Basnett)*

The *Tynwald* leaving the Queen's Pier at Ramsey for Douglas during July 1968. *(W.S. Basnett)*

Steam Packet Winter

Top:- The *Mona's Isle* arriving at Peel after having been diverted from Douglas during easterly gales in February 1966.
(W.S. Basnett)

Middle:- The *Manxman* (Captain Tom Corteen) leaving Douglas in an easterly gale during December 1968.
(W.S. Basnett)

Below:- Easter 1975 saw the *King Orry* covered in six inches of snow at the Liverpool Landing Stage. *(John Shepherd)*

Holland. This contract would run until February 1949.

On Tuesday, 11th November 1947 the *King Orry* picked up two survivors from the schooner *Ellie Park* which had foundered in a full south-westerly gale on passage from Douglas to Connah's Quay.

1948

During the winter overhaul period, a flying bridge was built above the wheelhouse on the *King Orry* and *Mona's Queen*. This was used when the vessel was manoeuvring astern, and was extended to the full width of the ship at the next overhaul.

The *Snaefell* [5] was launched at Birkenhead on 3rd March 1948, and ran her trials on the Clyde on 20th July when she attained 21.80 knots. Her maiden voyage was from Liverpool to Douglas on 24th July.

In 1948 no consideration was given to adjusting departure times from Douglas to suit tidal conditions at Fleetwood. The steamer would leave Douglas at 16.00 and if necessary steam at slow speed to avoid arriving at the Wyre Light at low water. Passages of up to five hours took place on occasions, and many minor groundings in the Wyre Channel are recorded.

Between 19th and 24th September, the new *Snaefell* made a series of evening cruises from Fleetwood along the coast to Blackpool to view the illuminations, which in 1948 had been newly restored after the war.

The *Mona's Isle* [4] was sold for breaking up in October, and left Douglas under tow of the tugs *Strongbow* and *Warrior* bound for Milford Haven where the old ship ended her days.

On the morning of Christmas Day 1948 the *King Orry's* midnight departure from Liverpool was delayed until 02.25 – 'waiting for the arrival of trains'.

1949

The *Manxman's* contract with the British Government finished in 1949 and she left Harwich on 25th February to steam north. Under the command of Captain O. Taylor she was bound for Barrow, but due to severe storms she had to anchor overnight 27th/28th February in Ramsey Bay. After arriving at Barrow she is reported to have been surveyed with a view to further service, but the costs involved far outweighed her life expectancy. She was sold for scrap and left Barrow on 9th August 1949, under tow of the tug *Warrior* and was delivered to T.W. Ward's demolition berth at Preston.

During the 1949/50 winter work commenced on reblading the *Viking's* turbines as she lay in the Morpeth Dock, Birkenhead.

1950

The appearance of the *Ben-my-Chree* was further altered in 1950 with the removal of the cravat cowl from her funnel.

Services from Douglas to Dublin recommenced in 1950 for the first time since 1939. The *Snaefell* acted as tender to the Cunard liner *Ascania* in Douglas Bay on the occasion of the first Manx Homecoming after the war.

The annual Tynwald Fair Day excursion was from Peel to Belfast on Wednesday, 5th July. It was operated by the *King Orry* in perfect weather conditions, with a passage time of 3 hours 20 minutes. By contrast a similar excursion took place on Wednesday, 13th September and in a southerly force 9, the *King Orry* took 4 hours 42 mins to reach Peel from Belfast.

The sisters **Mona's Isle** [4] and **Victoria** (left) together at 'The Tongue' in March 1948. The 'Isle' was sold for scrap at the end of the season. *(Keith P. Lewis)*

Three days later on Saturday, 16th September, the *King Orry* left Fleetwood for Douglas at 15.31 and encountered SSE 8 conditions. Douglas harbour was unapproachable and so she went north to Ramsey Bay for shelter and anchored at 19.22. Her unfortunate passengers had to spend the night on board and, by morning, the wind was round to the WSW and blowing force 9. The 'Orry's' anchor was aweigh at 07.35 and after a stormy reduced speed passage of 1 hour 55 mins, she reached the south Edward Pier at 09.30 on Sunday, 17th September: 17 hours 59 mins after leaving Fleetwood.

The *Manx Maid's* final passenger sailing was from Liverpool to Douglas on 26th August, after which she was laid up at 'The Tongue'. On 12th November she was towed to Barrow for demolition by T.W. Ward & Company.

The fifth of the post war fleet replacements, the *Mona's Isle* [5], was launched from Cammell Laird's yard on 12th October. Work was completed on reblading the *Viking's* turbines.

1951

The new *Mona's Isle* [5] put into Douglas on Thursday, 15th March to pick up a party of Company officials who would be on board for her trials on the Clyde the following day. After successfully reaching 21.91 knots the new ship returned south, but a force 9 gale prevented her from entering Douglas and landing the trials party. She proceeded to Liverpool, only to become fogbound at the Mersey Bar, which caused her to anchor. When the fog cleared, the *Mona's Queen* was seen approaching on the regular morning sailing to Douglas and so the trials party were transferred from the 'Isle' to the 'Queen' in a motor lifeboat, and were duly returned to Douglas. The new 'Isle' then proceeded to Cammell Laird's wet basin and was handed over to the Steam Packet Company on 20th March. Her maiden voyage was from Liverpool to Douglas on 22nd March.

The *Tynwald* [3[/ *Western Isles/ Eastern Isles* left Wallasey Dock (where she had lain since 1939) at 07.30 on Wednesday, 13th May 1951. She was towed to La Spezia for demolition by the United Towing Company's *Airman*. The ship had been returned to her owner, Mr. Colby Cubbin, in 1947, but it would have cost an estimated £100,000 to put her back into service. She had been afloat for a remarkable sixty years.

A 'personal best' for the Liverpool and Douglas passage was made by the *King Orry* on Wednesday, 23rd May 1951. With Captain O. Taylor as Master and Mr. A.W.G. Kissack as

In March 1951, the *Mona's Isle* [5] entered service. *(FotoFlite)*

Mate, the 'Orry' left north Prince's Stage at 15.31, passed the Rock Light at 15.39, the Mersey Bar at 16.15, and was abeam Douglas Head at 18.41. She was alongside the south Edward Pier at 18.49, just 3 hours 18 mins after leaving Liverpool. Fast passages between Liverpool and Douglas were invariably made using the full effect of an ebb spring tide in the Mersey estuary.

For many years the cargo service from Coburg Dock at Liverpool had been operated by the *Conister* [1] and the *Peveril* [2]. A third vessel was often required and the Company had chartered the *Sybil Mary, Clara Monks, T P Tilling, Sprayville* and *Seaville* for various periods since the war. However, a new purpose-built cargo vessel was launched

at Troon on 6th August 1951. She was the *Fenella* [3] and was built by the Ailsa Shipbuilding Company: the first ship to be built in Scotland for the Company for 54 years. The *Fenella* was the Steam Packet's first motorship and entered service in December. This was not a moment too soon as the main chartered vessel, the *Seaville*, had sunk two weeks earlier near the Q.15 buoy in the Mersey approaches after being in collision with the *Mersey No 30,* a hopper barge of the Mersey Docks and Harbour Board.

The cargo berth at Douglas dried out at low tide, and the problem of keeping the *Fenella's* diesel generators cooled was solved by circulating the water from the ballast tanks.

The *King Orry,* usually the mainstay of the winter services,

On August Bank Holiday 1951, no less than eight Steam Packet passenger vessels were in Douglas Harbour. Outside on the Victoria Pier is the **Ben-my-Chree**; inside are the **Lady of Mann, Victoria, King Orry** and **Snaefell** with the **Viking** astern. On the north Edward Pier are the **Mona's Queen** and **Mona's Isle** while the Liverpool & North Wales Steamship Co's **St. Seiriol** lies on the south Edward. The cargo steamer **Conister** is berthed closest to the camera. *(IOMSPCo)*

The Company's first diesel-powered vessel was the cargo ship *Fenella* [3] which entered service in December 1951. *(W.S. Basnett)*

was laid up at Barrow from Sunday, 14th October 1951 until May 1952.

1952

Two mishaps occurred early in 1952. On 25th February the *Tynwald* sank the barge *Eleanor* in the Mersey, and a month later the *Mona's Queen* struck the Battery Pier when entering Douglas harbour.

The Steam Packet's passenger traffic had always been concentrated into summer peaks, and necessitated the Company keeping a large reserve of steamers for summer only use. Only two passenger vessels were required during the long winter months, and usually six units of the fleet would spend almost nine months of every year laid up at Barrow or Birkenhead.

The principal 'peak' was the weekend of the returning T.T. Week race traffic, when the entire fleet would operate a shuttle service around the clock, and the other peaks were the last two Saturdays in July, and the first three in August. Saturday, 2nd August 1952 was a typical busy day. Leaving Liverpool at 00.27 the *King Orry* had 2,160 passengers on board and on a return sailing from Douglas at 06.15, she carried 1,900. The 'Orry' departed from Liverpool again at 10.50 with her full complement of 2,160 passengers, and the day was rounded off with the 16.00 Douglas to Fleetwood sailing with 1,440 passengers: 7,660 passengers carried on one steamer in 24 hours.

1953

Saturday, 31st January 1953 produced one of the worst winter storms of the century. As usual the *King Orry* was on winter service and left Liverpool at 10.55 with 120 passengers. After passing the Rock Light she met NNW force 12

conditions and her log records 'very heavy broken sea, fierce rain and sleet squalls. Vessel pitching and pounding heavily, shipping much water at times'. (It will be recalled that, on this stormy day, the British Railways car ferry *Princess Victoria*, which had left Stranraer for Larne at 06.45, went down with heavy loss of life). The *King Orry* finally berthed at Douglas at 21.55, exactly eleven hours after leaving Liverpool.

In February 1953 the *Mona's Queen* developed serious boiler trouble and she had to return to Cammell Laird. This led to the Easter sailings being covered by just two steamers, instead of the traditional three.

The Heysham service was not reinstated after the war until the summer of 1953, and then with only seven sailings during the entire season. Heysham could produce some good passenger figures, and on Wednesday 5th August, 1,570 excursionists were on board despite indifferent weather – WSW force 5, a rather rough sea and overcast with squalls.

On Monday, 23rd November, the *Mona's Queen* had to go off service again with recurrent boiler trouble, and until Tuesday, 1st December the *King Orry* maintained the winter services alone, operating a 09.00 sailing from Douglas and a 15.00 return from Liverpool. The *Tynwald* appeared the next day and restored the sailings to their normal pattern.

One Michael Jay met the Steam Packet Board of Directors at their meeting on 26th November 1953, and said that he represented a group which intended to make an offer of £3 per share for the £1 shares. Mr. Jay promised to submit his proposals to the next full board meeting, but nothing more was heard from him. By the time of the next Annual General Meeting in February 1952, Mr. Jay had sold almost all his holding. However in 1954 the Company's capital was increased again by a bonus issue of three shares for two, bringing it up to £1,500,000.

1954

Gales from an easterly point always caused problems at Douglas until the new breakwater was completed in the early 1980s. There was no sheltered berth and at high tide a heavy swell would cause vessels to range up and down the pier. In ESE force 9 conditions on Wednesday, 27th January 1954, the *King Orry* sailed directly from Liverpool to Peel, and arrived at the sheltered west coast port at 15.56, after a passage of 5 hours 6 minutes. This was the first instance in post war years of Peel being used as a diversionary port for Douglas. Peel was regularly used in subsequent winters, and during the winter of 1978/79 eighteen diversions were made owing to Douglas being virtually unapproachable in easterly gales.

The *Mona's Queen* had continuing boiler trouble, and was given a major refit from January until March 1954, which included the installation of radar. She returned to service on Tuesday, 2nd March.

The *Viking's* final passages were made on the Fleetwood run on 14th August under the command of Captain J.E. Quirk. Her departure from Fleetwood was broadcast on that evening's B.B.C. Radio Newsreel. On the morning of 16th August, Captain Quirk took the old steamer out of Douglas for the last time bound for Barrow and the scrapyard of T W Ward & Company. The Viking was 49 years old, and in view of her long association with the Fleetwood service, her bell was presented to the Borough of Fleetwood at a ceremony held on 24th May 1955.

1955

The *Manxman* [2] was launched on 8th February 1955 from Cammell Laird's Birkenhead yard. Her trials took place on the Clyde on 12th May when a speed of 21.95 knots was achieved. The new ship was different from her five older sisters in that four of her lifeboats were carried in Welin

The *Viking* remained in service for 49 years but was retired after the 1954 season. *(Malcolm McRonald collection)*

gravity davits. Whilst this slightly detracted from her appearance, it removed the clutter on the boat deck which was a cause of criticism on the older ships. The *Manxman's* main engines were two Pametrada (Parsons and Marine Engineering Turbine Research and Development Association) steam turbines, each driving its associated propeller through double reduction gearing.

The *Manxman* sailed 'light' for Douglas on 20th May, and her maiden passenger sailing was, somewhat unusually, from Douglas to Liverpool on 21st May. After this she sailed 'light' for Fleetwood and opened the seasonal service on 23rd May – a worthy successor to the *Viking*. The new *Manxman* became the regular winter steamer along with the *King Orry*, and the *Mona's Queen* was henceforward used for relief winter sailings only.

In 1955 the Steam Packet's fleet consisted of six fine new steamers, plus the pre-war *Lady of Mann, Ben-my-Chree* and *Victoria*. The cargo services were operated by the *Fenella* [3], *Peveril* [2] and the *Conister*. The fleet had a total age of 202

The *Manxman* on winter service arriving at Peel in January 1972. *(W.S.Basnett)*

years, giving an average age per unit of 17 years. Ten out of the twelve ships had been built to Steam Packet specifications. The passenger steamers could together accommodate in excess of 19,000 passengers. Compare this to the situation that existed in 1945 when the average age of each ship in the fleet was 32 years.

The *Mona's Isle* was aground off Fleetwood at 01.45 on 8th June 1955 after a collision with the fishing vessel *Ludo*. The *Ludo* was cut in half and sank almost immediately, and one of her crew was lost. In the same month, the suction from the *King Orry* caused the Fleetwood ferry *Wyresdale* to be torn from her moorings.

1956

At the end of the 1956 summer season, the *Victoria* made her final passenger sailing from Douglas to Liverpool on 17th August. She left Douglas at 15.10 and made the passage in just 3 hours 18 minutes – good to the last. The Company's last two funnelled steamer entered the Wallasey Dock at Birkenhead and remained there until 25th January 1957 when, in her fiftieth year, the tug *Rosegarth* towed her to Barrow, and the breakers' yard.

Christmas Eve 1956 brought a south-easterly 8 gale, and the *King Orry* was diverted to Peel where she arrived at the breakwater at 17.10. There would be no rest for the ship over Christmas as the gale increased to force 9, and the *Manxman* needed to berth with the overnight sailing from Liverpool. There is only room for one steamer alongside Peel breakwater and so, at 09.42 on Christmas morning, the *King Orry* moved to an anchorage in Peel Bay to let the *Manxman* in. So bad were the conditions that the starboard anchor was also let go at noon. There were blizzard conditions throughout; visibility was reported in the log as being 'nil' in the snow.

1957

The *Manxman* was aground in the Mersey off Egremont on 8th September 1957 owing to an exceptionally low spring tide. The tug *William Lamey* stood by her but was not required.

The *Ben-my-Chree*, now thirty years old, spent the greater part of the 1957/58 winter in No 5 drydock at Cammell Laird's yard undergoing a major refit following her survey.

1958

Following the reduction of the passenger fleet from nine ships to eight after the *Victoria's* retirement in 1956, the Steam Packet Company had chartered the Liverpool & North Wales Steamship Company's *St. Seiriol* for peak Saturdays in the seasons of 1957 and 1958. The final occasion on which this charter took place was Saturday, 16th August 1958 when the *St. Seiriol* made an 09.00 sailing from Douglas to Liverpool.

The Company had stipulated that the *St. Seiriol's* Master, Captain Kennedy, must hold the Fleetwood Pilotage Certificate. The ship was rostered for Fleetwood crossings but in the event she was not required to make them due to insufficient traffic, and all her charter sailings were between Douglas and Liverpool.

The reliability of the turbine steamers was second to none. It was almost possible to set a clock by the comings and goings of the Isle of Man steamers as they passed the Rock Light.

The end for the *Victoria* came in August 1956. Here she is laid-up in 'The Tongue' at Douglas. She was broken up in her fiftieth year. *(Keith P. Lewis)*

However on Wednesday 3rd December 1958 the *King Orry* was unable to leave Liverpool due to a burst steam pipe in the engine room. This was the only occasion in a 30 year career involving 7,412 sailings and steaming 516,770 miles that she was unable to sail on schedule because of mechanical trouble. The passengers, cars and mails were transferred to the *Manxman* as soon as she arrived from Douglas before she made the extra return sailing.

1959

Following the 'Ben's' major refit of a year earlier, the *Lady of Mann* received a comprehensive overhaul at Birkenhead during the 1958/59 winter. The 'Lady' usually wintered at Barrow.

In the late 1950s, fog caused severe disruption to the winter sailing schedules. On Tuesday, 13th January, the *King Orry* left Douglas as usual at 09.02 in an easterly force 2 and smooth seas. At 11.55, owing to dense fog, she anchored one mile outside the Bar Light vessel. She remained there for the next twenty hours, and her Master, Captain Lyndhurst Callow, reported that, at times, he could not see the water from the bridge. The following morning, 14th January, the anchor was hove up at 08.18, and an attempt was made to move up the sea channels to Liverpool but it proved impossible and at 08.38 the anchor was down again. At 11.40 the *King Orry* got underway again with the visibility improving and berthed at south Prince's Stage at 13.02, just twenty-four hours late. The overall passage time was twenty-eight hours. Fog became less of a problem as the Clean Air Acts were enforced and as radar became more sophisticated.

On Tuesday, 7th April the Cammell Laird workforce went

The **Ben-my-Chree** [4] received a major refit during the winter of 1957/8. *(W.S. Basnett)*

on strike and remained 'out' until Wednesday, 24th June. The *King Orry* was trapped in No 4 drydock. The *Mona's Isle* and the *Ben-my-Chree* were sent to Troon for their annual overhauls.

In August 1959 the *Snaefell* was chartered by British Railways to replace the disabled *Cambria* on the Holyhead – Dun Laoghaire route. She consistently recorded faster passages than the B.R. motorship. The *Mona's Queen* collided with Prince's Stage on 19th August which cut short her seasonal sailings. After repairs she proceeded to winter lay-up in the Morpeth Dock. On 4th September the *Tynwald* carried the retiring Governor of the Isle of Man, Sir Ambrose Flux Dundas, from Douglas to Liverpool.

1960

At the Company's Annual General Meeting on 24th February 1960 it was announced that an order might be placed for a car ferry vessel. "The matter is under careful and earnest consideration," said Mr. J.F. Crellin, Chairman of the Directors.

The appearance of the winter steamers, the *Manxman* and the *King Orry*, was altered somewhat by an extension to the bridge deck being built on. This was twenty feet long on both sides of the funnel and provided additional stowage space for life rafts which the Company was now required to provide. When the life rafts were in position the funnels on these two steamers appeared shorter than those of the other units of the class.

Sudden changes of wind direction could make for sleepless nights for the crews of the winter steamers. After arriving at Douglas in a strong easterly on Tuesday, 19th November 1960, the *Manxman* was ordered to make for a safe

anchorage in Peel Bay. Late in the evening the gale veered to the SSW making conditions at Peel difficult, so, at 22.30, the *Manxman* sailed 'north-about' for an anchorage in Ramsey Bay from 01.10 until 06.25, arriving back in Douglas at 07.40. More circumnavigations of the Island were made sheltering from the weather than took place on 'Round the Island' pleasure cruises in the summer.

1961

In May 1961 the appearance of the *King Orry* was once again altered with the removal of the cravat cowl from her funnel. The cowl was literally rusting away and was not replaced. She was the only one of the post-war steamers to lose her cowl.

On Tuesday, 1st August the *Lady of Mann* had to return to Liverpool owing to a bomb scare. Two phone calls were received by the Liverpool Agents of the Company, Thomas Orford & Son, and Captain G.R. Kinley was informed. The 'Lady' was approaching the Bar when Captain Kinley decided to return to Liverpool so that the ship could be searched.

At the end of the season the *St. Seiriol* was retired from service after maintaining the Llandudno to Douglas link since 1931. Her final passage was from Douglas to Llandudno on Wednesday, 6th September. The Steam Packet Company said that it would provide limited sailings on the route in 1962.

On Monday, 11th September the *Mona's Queen* took the final sailing from Fleetwood to Douglas before the Steam Packet abandoned the route as the wooden berth at Fleetwood was in a state of serious disrepair. The British Transport Commission had decided that the £750,000 cost of rebuilding the crumbling quay was not justified considering the return from passenger dues. With flags on the *Mona's*

Queen's foremast spelling out 'Deeply Regret Fleetwood Goodbye' she sailed at 10.30 with 1,193 passengers, many of them members of the Contractors' Club of the 'Poor Man's *Caronia*', who for £15, spent the summer sailing between Fleetwood and Douglas. For the record, the final Douglas to Fleetwood sailing was taken at 16.00 by the *Mona's Isle* and, after disembarking, she sailed immediately 'light ship' for Barrow.

The *Mona's Queen's* final sailing for the Company was from Douglas to Liverpool on Saturday, 16th September, after which she was laid up at Barrow and offered for sale. The closure of Fleetwood and the entry into service in 1962 of the new car ferry had made her redundant. Additional factors which sealed her fate were her history of boiler trouble and the fact that she had not been fitted for the winter crossings, as had the *King Orry*.

The closing days of 1961 saw the *King Orry* affected by two incidents. Firstly she was struck by the Mersey ferry *Royal Daffodil II* on Wednesday, 20th December in dense fog, causing extensive damage to her stern. The second incident occurred at 08.10 on the morning of Christmas Eve, Sunday 24th December, as she was attempting to enter Douglas harbour in a full easterly gale. The *King Orry* was between the pier heads when the gale caught her, and she fell very heavily on to the south corner of the Victoria Pier, splintering her main belting. Repairs were carried out by Cammell Laird but the ship's days as winter steamer were almost over: she would be superseded by the new car ferry in 1962.

CHAPTER 7
THE SIDE LOADING CAR FERRIES 1962 – 1977

The Steam Packet Company's first car ferry, the *Manx Maid* [2], was launched from Cammell Laird's yard on 23rd January 1962. The design principle for vehicle loading was simple – a spiral set of ramps at the stern linked with the car deck so that vehicles could be driven on or off at the appropriate level. This overcame the problem of the twenty foot tidal range at Douglas. At Liverpool the car deck was on the level with the landing stage. This system of inclined ramps was devised by the Company's superintendent Engineer, the late Mr. C.J. Kenna. The system had been used at least once before – on the Belgian car ferry *London-Istanbul*, ex *Ville de Liege*, introduced on the Dover to Ostend route in 1936.

The new *Manx Maid* ran her trials on the Clyde on 18th – 19th May, and her maiden voyage was from Liverpool to Douglas on 23rd May. Just on sailing time the north westerly breeze increased to gale force in gusts and the new steamer was pinned against the landing stage. The tugs *Pea Cock* and *Flying Cock* hauled her off the stage and the 'Maid' swept

Three of a kind on the north Edward Pier at Douglas. From left to right: the **Mona's Isle**, **Snaefell** and **Manxman**. *(W.S. Basnett)*

The first car ferry, the *Manx Maid* [2], slides down the ways towards the Mersey after her launch at Cammell Laird in January 1962. *(IOMSPCo)*

The **Manx Maid** enters the river for the first time. *(IOMSPCo)*

triumphantly through the turbulent waters of the Mersey to the traditional send-off from other vessels on the river. The *Manx Maid* was the first Steam Packet vessel to be fitted with stabilizers, and although she undoubtedly was a lively seaboat, some accounts of rough crossings have been grossly over-sensationalized.

In her first season the 'Maid' was used exclusively on the Liverpool and Douglas route.

Sunday, 16th September 1962 was the final occasion on which the *St. Tudno* operated the Liverpool – Llandudno – Menai Bridge sailings for the Liverpool & North Wales Steamship Company. Shortly afterwards the North Wales Company went into liquidation, and the Steam Packet quickly stepped in, stating that they would offer a limited Liverpool to Llandudno service in 1963, although their steamers were too large to make the sailing to Menai Bridge. Throughout the 1962 season the Company had operated a twice weekly Llandudno – Douglas service following the *St. Seiriol's* retirement.

In October the *Mona's Queen* [4] was sold to the Marivic Navigation Inc. of Monrovia (part of the Chandris group), and was renamed *Barrow Queen* for the passage to Piraeus. She left Barrow on 12th November with a Greek crew and a retired Isle of Man Steam Packet Company Chief Engineer, but on the following day put into Birkenhead with engine trouble. The *Barrow Queen* sailed for Piraeus on 14th November, and after a complete refit at Ambelaki, as the *Fiesta* she cruised the Mediterranean for almost 19 years.

1963

On Whit Sunday, 2nd June 1963, the *King Orry* operated the Steam Packet's first ever excursion sailing from Liverpool to Llandudno with 705 passengers. One of the problems of approaching Llandudno Pier at low water was immediately highlighted when one of the 'Orry's' propellers struck a boulder on the sea bed, which meant that she had to retire to Herculaneum Graving Dock to have the propeller changed.

The *Peveril* [2] had the suffix II added to her name in October so that the name could be given to a new cargo vessel which was being built at the Ailsa Yard at Troon. The third *Peveril* was launched on 3rd December 1963.

1964

In February 1964 the *Mona's Isle* was, somewhat unusually, on winter service and on Friday, 14th, she had been diverted to Peel because of an easterly gale. It was the usual practice, providing the gale had abated, for the steamer to sail around to Douglas early in the morning to pick up the 09.00 sailing, thus saving the inconvenience of having to bus the passengers across to Peel. The *Mona's Isle* had left Peel breakwater at 06.20 on Saturday, 15th February and shortly afterwards her stern ran aground on the rocks behind Peel Castle, severely damaging her rudder and propellers. The fishing boats *Signora* and *Yukon Fisher* were alerted and they towed the 'Isle' off the rocks on a rising tide, and took her to a safe anchorage in Peel Bay. In the evening the Liverpool tugs *North End* and *North Wall* arrived to tow the disabled steamer to Liverpool for drydocking and repairs. Extensive engine damage meant that the *Mona's Isle* did not resume service until 14th July, leaving the Company short of one ship during T.T. week.

The new purpose built cargo vessel *Peveril* [3] arrived at Douglas from Troon on 7th March 1964 and on the following day sailed on her maiden voyage to Liverpool. As

The *Manx Maid*

Top:-Seen here on builders' trials in the Firth of Clyde, the ***Manx Maid*** is running full astern. *(IOMSPCo)*

Left:- The vehicle deck looking astern.*(IOMSPCo)*

Below:-The wheelhouse. *(IOMSPCo)*

Steam Car Ferries

Top:- The 'Ben' leaving Douglas in the tail of a south easterly gale in January 1974. *(W.S. Basnett)*

Middle:- The **Ben-my-Chree** arriving at Liverpool in June 1974. *(Malcolm McRonald)*

Below:- The **Manx Maid** leaving Douglas in cold, blustery, weather in April 1981. *(W.S. Basnett)*

The *Manxman* (Captain Bernard Quirk) steaming stern first up Belfast Lough in August 1982. *(W.S. Basnett)*

Manx Maid

Top:- The Main Lounge.
(*IOMSPCo*)

Middle:- The Second Class
Lounge. (*IOMSPCo*)

Below:- The First Class Ladies
Lounge. (*IOMSPCo*)

Above and Below: In March 1964, the cargo steamer *Peveril* [2] was replaced by the diesel vessel *Peveril* [3]. *(both W.S. Basnett)*

More changes in the cargo fleet occurred in 1965 when the 44 year old single hatch coaster, **Conister** was towed away for scrap. *(W.S. Basnett)*

built, the *Peveril* was equipped with two 10 ton electric cranes. The old *Peveril II* arrived at Glasson Dock for breaking up on 29th May 1964.

On Monday, 3rd August 1,900 passengers arrived at Douglas on the 'Counties Charter' excursion from Dublin. Such high passenger numbers were not often carried on scheduled services, but mainly on the charter sailings and, given fair weather, on the Company's advertised excursions. The main problem for the Company was to occupy a fleet of eight steamers which were really only needed for certain peak Saturdays and to cope with the intensive T.T. motorcycle traffic.

1965

The 44 year old cargo steamer *Conister* was sold to Arnott Young & Company of Dalmuir for scrapping, and left Douglas under tow of the tug *Campaigner* on 26th January 1965.

To replace the *Conister* the Ailsa Shipbuilding Company delivered the small cargo vessel *Ramsey*, and she arrived in her 'home' port of Ramsey on 28th January to be welcomed by the Chairman of the town's Commissioners. This small motor

The **Conister** was replaced by the **Ramsey**. *(J.K. Byass)*

Left:- The **Ben-my-Chree** [4] at Liverpool prior to her last passenger sailing from the port - a charter to Belfast - on 11th September 1965. *(Keith P. Lewis)*

were severely damaged, resulting in the dramatic and violent release of impounded water!

The Barrow Round Table chartered the *Mona's Isle* for a day excursion to Llandudno on 27th June, and on 4th July the Blue Funnel Line chartered the *Snaefell* for a celebratory cruise for their staff from Liverpool to Llandudno. It had been suggested that the ship's funnel be painted blue for the occasion, but in the event she just flew the Alfred Holt houseflag at her foremast.

The final sailing of the *Ben-my-Chree* [4] was from Douglas to Liverpool in the early hours of Monday, 13th September 1965. At about 22.30 on the Sunday evening, the General Manager, Mr. Arthur J. Fick, had invited all of the 156 passengers into the first class dining saloon and after a short speech champagne was provided to 'toast' the old ship. The 'Ben' sailed at 00.03 and took a leisurely five hours for the passage to Liverpool. She was laid up in the Morpeth Dock and offered for sale. The suffix II was added to her name.

The new *Ben-my-Chree* [5] was launched from Cammell Laird's on Friday, 10th December 1965. She was the fourteenth (and final) ship to be built for the Steam Packet Company at Birkenhead. She was also the last steamer and the last vessel to be built with her passenger accommodation designed for two classes. There was almost an historic meeting on the Mersey that December day for the old 'Ben' should have left Birkenhead for the breakers' yard in Belgium on the same high tide that the new 'Ben' was launched.

Gales had delayed the arrival of the tug *Fairplay XI*, and it was not until dusk on Saturday, 18th December that the old

ship had crew accommodation for 18, which seems lavish by today's standards. Her maiden voyage was from Douglas to Liverpool on 2nd February.

On 19th March the *Peveril* [3] had left the Company's cargo berth at Coburg Dock and was approaching the Brunswick Lock, Liverpool, when her engines failed to respond to telegraphed orders from the bridge. The lock gates

The car ferry **Ben-my-Chree** at her best, going astern out of Douglas. *(W.S.Basnett)*

A dramatic view of the car ferry *Ben-my-Chree* leaving Douglas. Her passengers were in for a rough crossing! *(W.S. Basnett)*

'Ben' entered the Mersey for the last time and was towed to Van Heyghen's yard at Ghent, where she arrived on 23rd December, for demolition.

1966

The new *Ben-my-Chree* [5], the Company's second car ferry, ran her trials on the Clyde on 10th May 1966 and her maiden voyage was from Liverpool to Douglas on the afternoon of Thursday, 12th May. Apart from minor differences, most of which would have been difficult for the average traveller to spot, she was a 'repeat' of the highly successful *Manx Maid*. On the maiden voyage passengers were invited to inspect the bridge, and an excellent High Tea could be taken for 9s.6d. (47.5p).

On Sunday, 15th May the new steamer operated a 'Round the Island' excursion at a fare of 10/- (50p) which proved so popular that many intending passengers were turned away. This happy event was overshadowed by the threat of a seamen's strike, and after completing the excursion sailing, the 'Ben' immediately sailed 'light' to Barrow where she was laid up for the strike's 42 days duration.

Apart from the occasional 'mercy' sailings permitted by the National Union of Seamen and operated by the *Peveril*, the entire fleet was strikebound until Saturday, 2nd July, when sailings resumed with the two car ferries, the *Manxman* and the *Mona's Isle*. The economy of the Isle of Man was very seriously affected and the annual T.T. motorcycle races, always the Steam Packet's busiest period, were postponed until late August and attracted considerably less traffic than in the usual early June period.

On 9th September the *Ben-my-Chree* sailed from Ardrossan to Douglas in 4 hours 50 minutes, beating the previous record for the passage.

1967

During the winter of 1966-67 no Steam Packet vessels were laid up at Barrow for the first time in very many years.

With effect from 1st January 1967 all the Company's steamers became 'one-class' ships for passengers. Considerable savings could be effected by reducing the number of stewards, especially in the winter months.

Ronagency Shipping was formed in 1967 for the purpose of introducing a completely new and novel unit load and containerized shipping link to Castletown from Glasson Dock. The Steam Packet's cargo services still consisted entirely of break bulk shipments involving costly and time-consuming loading and discharging operations. Ronagency was the forerunner of Manx Line, a decade later.

The *Manx Maid* developed steering trouble on 22nd July 1967 and entered the Mersey stern first.

Llandudno Pier was not available to the Company in 1967 as the wooden berthing head was falling into serious disrepair. Whilst not as important as Fleetwood had been, Llandudno nevertheless produced some 30,000 day-trippers every season, and together with the Liverpool to Llandudno sailings provided valuable mid-week employment for the Company's steamers. Negotiations between the Steam Packet and Llandudno Pier Company led to the construction of two concrete dolphins at the end of the pier. The steamers would tie up alongside these dolphins (mooring posts), rather than against the structure itself. The cost was £36,000 and the work was completed by the end of May 1968.

1968

The *Manx Maid* suffered a further steering failure on 17th February 1968 when abeam the Q.17 buoy in the Queen's Channel in the Mersey approaches, and had to be towed back to Liverpool by the Alexandra tugs *Trafalgar* and *North Wall*.

Douglas Harbour

Top:- Ready for the mass exodus. The *King Orry, Manxman, Ben-my-Chree, Lady of Mann* (all on the Victoria Pier), *Tynwald, Mona's Isle, Snaefell* (on the Edward Pier) and the cargo vessel *Peveril* during TT Week 1965. *(W.S. Basnett)*

Middle:- The ro-ro freighter *Peveril* at the Edward Pier linkspan in September 1968. *(John Hendy)*

Left:- Opposition ! The *Norwest Laird* arriving at Douglas in July 1970 while the *Snaefell* and the *Manx Maid* lay-by on the Victoria Pier. *(Malcolm McRonald)*

The Norwegian vessel *Stella Marina* operated a Fleetwood-Douglas service from Easter until September 1969. *(Raymond Brandreth collection)*

The Liverpool to Llandudno sailings taken over from the Liverpool & North Wales Steamship Company in 1963 never really came up to expectations, and can hardly have been profitable. The motor car was on the rapid increase in the 1960s and families seemed to prefer sitting in endless queues on the Queensferry by-pass, on the main trunk road from Merseyside to North Wales, rather than enjoying fresh sea air on the deck of a steamer. The Company was also reluctant to advertise the sailings in the traditional catchment area. Four hundred passengers was a good loading and at least 100 of those would be contract ticket holders from the old *St. Tudno* days.

1969

The sea link between Douglas and Fleetwood reopened on Good Friday, 4th April 1969 when Norwest Hovercraft Limited placed the 700 passenger, 1,339 ton *Stella Marina* on the route. A daily round trip, increased to two on Saturdays, was planned.

The British Rail vehicle ferry *Antrim Princess* made a special charter sailing from Stranraer to Douglas in May – her first visit to the Isle of Man. Sixteen years later, this vessel would become the Steam Packet's *Tynwald* [6].

In 1969 the Company moved into its new purpose built head office opposite the sea terminal at Douglas. In the course of the transfer from the old Imperial Buildings (formerly the Imperial Hotel), large amounts of old documents were destroyed and burned in quayside bonfires. If only they could have been preserved, they would have been of incalculable benefit to today's historians.

Throughout the year the cargo service was disrupted by strikes and shortages of labour at Liverpool. Although three cargo vessels were available, the service was held up by five strikes at Liverpool resulting in delays and a large increase in costs. Runcorn was used as an alternative whenever possible.

1970

A prolonged strike of Mersey tugmen in early 1970 caused problems in the Steam Packet's drydocking and overhaul schedules. In May Captain Corteen brought the *Lady of Mann* into Liverpool from Barrow, manoeuvred her through the locks and passages, and docked her in the Langton Graving Dock. Ten days later he undocked her, again without the assistance of tugs. Captain Corteen took the 'Lady' to Llandudno on the annual Tynwald Fair Day excursion from

Douglas on 6th July. Her first ever visit to the Welsh resort had taken place seven days earlier on 30th June.

In 1970 an afternoon cruise from Llandudno Pier was introduced whenever the Liverpool to Llandudno sailings operated. From 1963 until 1969 P.& A. Campbell had placed the *St. Trillo* on short cruises at Llandudno, but on her withdrawal, the Steam Packet inaugurated a two hour cruise to Puffin Island and along the Anglesey coast towards Point Lynas. These cruises became increasingly popular, and given fair weather regularly carried upwards of 1,500 passengers thanks in no small part to the efforts of the Company's Llandudno Agent, Gerry Bouwman.

The 1970 Fleetwood to Douglas service operated by Norwest Shipping was a fiasco to say the least. Unable to charter the *Stella Marina*, the company eventually placed the elderly *Norwest Laird* on the link. This vessel had been built for David MacBrayne Limited in 1939 as the *Lochiel* and was of 603 tons gross, 58.22 metres in length and had a speed of 13 knots. Norwest Shipping themselves stated that she was 'too small to be comfortable for passengers'. Had the *Stella Marina* been available in 1970, the *Norwest Laird* would have been used on a Barrow – Fleetwood – Morecambe service. The *Norwest Laird* eventually entered service several weeks late because of a dispute with Cammell Laird and engine trouble. She sailed with a Class III certificate which meant that she had to stay within regulation distance of land, (20 miles), involving a circuitous passage towards St. Bees Head. By way of this route, she took upwards of six hours between Fleetwood and Douglas. Only fourteen round trips were completed and mishaps abounded: on one occasion she ran aground on a sandbank at Fleetwood during a midnight sailing to Douglas and the 63 passengers had to be taken off by lifeboat; on another the *Norwest Laird* developed engine trouble at Douglas and a Cambrian Airways' Viscount had to be chartered to get the day-excursion passengers off the Island.

It was announced in late August 1970 that Ramsey's Queen's Pier would be closed to passenger vessels at the end of the season. The wooden berthing head was in very poor condition and the estimated cost of a replacement was £60,000. In the previous twenty years over £130,000 had been spent on maintenance of the pier, whilst just under £15,000 had been produced by passenger dues. In 1906, 36,000 passengers had been embarked or were landed at the pier: in 1969 this figure was down to 3,054. Mr. Shimmin, the Steam Packet's General Manager commented: "It will simply be a loss of convenience to some passengers." The final occasion on which a Steam Packet vessel called at Ramsey Pier was on Thursday, 10th September 1970 when the *Manxman* berthed alongside on the Belfast sailing.

1971

Sunday, 13th June 1971 was the last day of the busy T.T. shuttle service following the annual motorcycle races. The *King Orry* had left Douglas at 09.30 with 490 passengers, 16 cars and 180 motorcycles. At 11.19 she received a message to reduce speed because the port of Liverpool was closed to all shipping following a serious leakage of highly volatile chemicals at Bromborough. Rather than return to Douglas where she would have aggravated an already hectic situation, at 12.26 the 'Orry' was ordered to proceed to Ardrossan and course was altered from S.36 E to N.21 W. Quite what was

1970 saw the closure of the Queen's Pier at Ramsey to Steam Packet vessels. The *Tynwald* is seen there in August 1968. *(W.S. Basnett)*

Diesel Car Ferries

Top:- The *Mona's Queen* leaving Douglas for Stranraer in September 1988 while the Laxey Towing Company's *Salisbury* berths at the Battery Pier. *(John Hendy)*

Below:- The *Lady of Mann* arriving at Douglas from Belfast in June 1994. *(Miles Cowsill)*

In Disguise

Top:- In her final season, the *Manxman* was chartered to a movie company to star in the film 'Yentl'. Here the Russian immigrant carrier *Moskva* arrives at the Landing Stage after a day's shooting in Liverpool Bay.
(J.R. Clague)

Middle:- Who would guess that the vessel nearest the camera was once the Steam Packet's *Mona's Queen* [4]. Here she is as the *Fiesta* at Piraeus in July 1970.
(Malcolm McRonald)

Below:- On 2nd September 1989, the *Mona's Queen* [5] was chartered by the French Post Office to support their *La Poste* at the start of the Round the World Yacht Race. The 'Queen' is seen leaving Portsmouth for Cherbourg later that afternoon. *(John Hendy)*

In August 1971, the forty one year old **Lady of Mann** was retired from the fleet. Here she is looking at her best, arriving at Douglas in some breezy summer sunshine. *(W.S. Basnett)*

the reaction of the passengers to this turn of events is not recorded in the log! The situation at Liverpool improved, however, and although the upper reaches of the Mersey remained closed, the section from Prince's Stage seawards was re-opened to traffic. At 13.15 the *King Orry* resumed her original course to Liverpool and arrived at 15.07 (a passage of 6 hours 4 minutes).

Arguably the Steam Packet's most famous steamer, the magnificent *Lady of Mann* of 1930 was nearing the end of her career in 1971. On the evening of Thursday, 12th August the Company arranged a farewell cruise. Drizzling rain, clammy mist and choppy grey seas put holidaymakers off this 'pleasure' cruise from Douglas to the Calf of Man but they didn't put off the Manx who would have gone in a hurricane!

The 'Lady's' final passenger sailing was from Ardrossan to Douglas on the afternoon of Sunday, 14th August. A large crowd had gathered on the Point of Ayre, the northernmost tip of the Isle of Man, to watch her steam majestically by at 16.45; the Ramsey coastguards sent up flares and the lighthouse keepers at Maughold Head saluted her with the mournful note of the fog syren.

The *Lady of Mann* left Douglas for the last time at 17.00 on Tuesday, 17th August on her way to Barrow to lay up, pending sale. In perfect weather the piers and promenades were lined with several thousand people who wished the old ship an emotional farewell as she swept passed the harbour entrance to the accompaniment of her triple chime whistle.

The 'Lady' lay at her birthplace, Barrow, until the end of the year. She was purchased by Arnott Young of Dalmuir for demolition, and arrived there on the last day of 1971 under tow of the tug *Wrestler*.

The port of Fleetwood reopened to Manx steamers on Wednesday, 25th August. A new berth, capable of accommodating the Company's vessels, had been constructed, and appropriately the *Mona's Isle* was rostered to open the new service. This same steamer had worked the final Douglas to Fleetwood sailing ten years earlier. A daily service was offered until Thursday, 2nd September with a day-return fare of £2.50p.

It was agreed by Royal Warrant in October 1971 that Steam Packet ships, indeed any vessels registered in the Isle of Man, could in future fly the red ensign defaced by the emblem of the three Legs of Man.

In the summer of 1971 there had been an acute shortage of car space, and the passenger steamers frequently duplicated the car ferry sailings, carrying a full load of cars and their mere eighty or so passengers. When carrying cars on the shelter deck of passenger steamers, an allowance had to be made to the passenger complement on the basis of one less passenger for each six square feet of space taken up by cars. In effect this meant that if 16 cars were carried, then 500 fewer passengers could be carried. This situation would be resolved in 1972 with the entry into service of the Company's third car-ferry, and the *Mona's Queen* [5] was named at the Ailsa Yard at Troon on 21st December. Owing to gales it was not considered safe to launch her until the following day.

1972

The *Peveril* [3] was converted to a container ship by her builders when the cranes were removed and a cellular system for 56 twenty foot equivalent units (TEUs) was installed. The container revolution rapidly changed the Company's cargo services. At Douglas a 28-ton derrick crane was erected on the site of the Company's old head office building to handle the containers. The weekly Ramsey freight sailing was withdrawn in 1972 and the cargo vessel *Ramsey*, which had made her

The launch, at Troon, of the **Mona's Queen** [5] in December 1971. *(IOMSPCo)*

maiden voyage as recently as February 1965, was effectively redundant as was the *Fenella* of 1951.

On 9th June 1972 the *Mona's Queen* [5] made her maiden voyage from Liverpool to Douglas. Eight days later the Alexandra tugs *Formby* and *Collingwood* towed her into the Gladstone Dock at Liverpool because of engine trouble. Unfortunately this was to be a rather frequent occurrence in her first few months of service.

The new 'Queen' was the Steam Packet Company's first diesel passenger ship, and the first to be constructed for one class of passengers. She was also the first Company vessel to be fitted with a bow-thrust unit, which greatly assisted in speeding up berthing times.

The entry into service of the *Mona's Queen* meant that for the first time, continuous car-ferry working could be maintained during the winter months. Up to to the 1971 –

The **Mona's Queen** was the Company's first diesel-driven car ferry. *(W.S. Basnett)*

The car ferries *Lady of Mann* and *Mona's Queen* laid up in Birkenhead's Vittoria Dock at Easter 1992. *(John Hendy)*

The *Spaniel* was chartered in 1973 and later purchased by the Company. She was renamed *Conister* [2]. *(W.S. Basnett)*

1972 winter, the *Manxman* had been pressed into winter service whilst the *Manx Maid* and the *Ben-my-Chree* received their annual overhauls. Carrying large numbers of cars on the *Manxman* and her sisters always caused severe clutter on the shelter deck and inconvenience for passengers; it also involved removing the Company's time honoured bench type seating – a laborious and time consuming job for the deck crew. Unless the vessel was 'on the level' at Douglas at high water, vehicles had to be craned on and off, necessitating cars for shipment being available alongside the steamer at 07.30 for a 09.00 sailing. This was not always appreciated by car-drivers who had become more and more used to the convenience of the car-ferries over the previous ten years.

The southern system of docks at Liverpool was closed in September 1972 and the Company's cargo berth was transferred from Coburg Dock to Hornby Dock where there was ample space for container handling and storage. The *Fenella* left Douglas for the last time on 27th December and later that day was laid up with the passenger steamers in the Morpeth Dock at Birkenhead. She was offered for sale and was quickly sold to the Cypriot Juliet Shipping Company, and left the Mersey on 9th February 1973 as the *Vasso M* for further trading in the eastern Mediterranean.

1973

The Steam Packet Company chartered the *Spaniel* from the Belfast S.S. Company in 1973 and then bought her outright in November and renamed her *Conister* [2]. The vessel had been built by George Brown (Marine) Limited in 1955 as the *Brentfield* for the Zillah Shipping Company of Liverpool, and in 1959 her name was changed to *Spaniel* following her conversion to a container ship for Link Line, part of the Coast Lines Group. The Ailsa Shipbuilding

Company of Troon adapted her to the requirements of the Steam Packet Company, and she was able to carry 46 TEUs.

With the advent of the *Spaniel*, the *Ramsey* became redundant and was sent to her home port to lay up. Later in the year the *Ramsey* moved to the Morpeth Dock, and it was there that she was purchased by R. Lapthorn & Company of Rochester, at a price well below her book value. She was renamed *Hoofort* and left Birkenhead on 9th January 1974 for further trading on the south coast.

On Sunday, 2nd September the Liverpool to Llandudno excursion sailings were operated for the first and last time by the car-ferry *Ben-my-Chree*. In the afternoon the 'Ben' took the afternoon cruise along the Anglesey coast.

The Liverpool Landing Stage was rapidly falling into disrepair in 1973. At the south end of the stage the damage sustained when the *Snaefell* went astern into it in fog on Monday, 9th March 1970 was never properly repaired. The Atlantic liners had all left the port and the Customs and Immigration sheds were vandalised and derelict. A new and much smaller stage was planned but the cost of this was escalating in the inflationary early 70s from £800,000 in October 1971 to £1.25 million in February 1973.

1974

Over the winter months of 1973/74 the price of fuel oil had quadrupled. In October 1973 the Company was paying £8 per ton, and in February 1974 this had risen to £34 per ton. The Company's sailing brochures had been printed and distributed showing a 1974 return fare of £7.20p, just 60p up on 1973, but in view of the oil price increases it was found necessary to impose surcharges and, with effect from 13th February, the return fare became £9, a massive 36% rise over 1973.

In 1974, the *Mona's Queen* inaugurated car-ferry sailings to Dublin.

Although it was not known at the time, the last week of August provided two 'final occasions'. On Bank Holiday Monday, 26th August, the *King Orry* brought a special excursion sailing from Liverpool with 490 passengers, arriving at 13.20. A few minutes later the *Tynwald* arrived from Llandudno. For just over two hours there were seven Steam Packet passenger vessels in Douglas Harbour, the last time this would ever happen as the *Tynwald* was sold at the end of the year.

Two days later, on 28th August, the final sailings were made on the Heysham route with the *King Orry* outward to Douglas, and the *Mona's Isle* on the return to Heysham. The Company announced that there was 'insufficient passenger potential to meet the additional operating costs' on the Heysham route. Not even the most imaginative fortune-teller could have visualized the events of a decade later!

In October the *Tynwald* was placed in the hands of brokers for sale following extensive damage to one of her turbines during the season. She was sold to John Cashmore of Newport, Gwent, for £57,000 and re-sold to Spanish shipbreakers at Aviles. The tug *Sea Bristolian* towed the *Tynwald* out of the Mersey on 3rd February 1975. Before she left, her triple chime whistle was removed, and this was eventually fitted to the *Ben-my-Chree* in 1978, replacing a particularly weak sounding horn type whistle.

On Wednesday, 13th November 1974 the *Manx Maid* hit

The cargo vessel **Conister** [2] arriving at Douglas with a deck full of containers. *(W.S. Basnett)*

the Fort Anne jetty whilst arriving in Douglas in bad weather. The 'Maid' was attempting to berth at the south Edward Pier, but the river was in spate following prolonged rainfall, and the strong current pushed her against the jetty, causing damage to her stem and bow rudder. She was taken out of service, and after warping round the end of the Edward Pier, she sailed the next day for repairs at Birkenhead.

The extreme northern section of the Liverpool landing stage sank during a severe December storm, taking with it the Company's booking office. The Mersey Docks and Harbour Company modified a section of the mid-stage for use in 1975.

1975

The year opened with the *Manx Maid* trapped in a Birkenhead dry dock. An industrial dispute had broken out after she had entered the dock and, for six months, the car-ferry was unable to leave. In February it was announced that the new landing stage would cost an additional £500,000 bringing the total to £1.75 million.

The 1975 summer season turned out to be a very successful one for the Company. The weather was superb throughout, much fresher and clearer than the oppressively hot summer of 1976. On Saturday, 24th May the *Manx Maid* finally emerged from the dry dock and immediately re-entered service. The annual Tynwald Fair Day excursion from Douglas to Llandudno attracted 1,823 Manx people. Co-op Charter day, Wednesday, 23rd July, was notable in that it was the final occasion on which three Manx steamers would berth together on Prince's Stage: from north to south they were the *Manx Maid, Manxman* and *King Orry*. The Stranraer to Douglas excursion on Sunday, 27th July carried 1,630 passengers. On Tuesday, 29th July, 1,948 passengers arrived from Fleetwood, and a further 2,005 from Llandudno. In this glorious summer the inevitable happened on Wednesday, 30th July when the *Snaefell* had to leave 300 intending passengers behind at Fleetwood.

The total number of passengers carried by the Company in 1975 amounted to 909,556; the highest for many years and a total which has not been exceeded since, nor is it ever likely to be.

The *King Orry's* final passenger sailings took place on Sunday, 31st August when she operated the Liverpool to Llandudno excursion. On arrival back from the afternoon cruise, Llandudno Pier had been dressed with flags and the notice at the end of the pier read, 'This steamer returns to Liverpool at 5.15 for the last time'. Press photographs were taken and at 17.20 the *King Orry* sailed on her 7,412th and final sailing for the Company. In the course of a remarkable thirty year career the old ship had steamed 516,770 miles and carried 3,325,500 passengers.

In October the *King Orry* was sold to R. Taylor & Sons of Bury, who intended to break her up at Glasson Dock, near Lancaster. She left Birkenhead under tow of the tug *Sea Bristolian* in the late evening of 4th November. It was an eventful tow and tragically a seaman on the tug was killed when he was struck by the towing hawser. In the Lune Deep, off Fleetwood, the 'Orry' broke away from the tow and the flood tide carried her down on to two anchored tugs. She eventually reached Glasson Dock at 13.00 on 5th November.

The Company's fourth car-ferry, the *Lady of Mann* [2] was launched from the Troon yard of the Ailsa Shipbuilding Company on 4th December 1975. For the first time, the car-ferries outnumbered the classic passenger steamers in the Company's fleet.

1976

During the severe north-westerly storm on the evening of 2nd January 1976 the *King Orry* [4] broke adrift from her berth at Glasson Dock and grounded in the Lune Estuary on the top of a very high tide, made even higher by the storm surge. She became something of a tourist attraction but her buyers were determined to refloat her. Weeks of patient work involving digging away the sand from around the hull brought results on 14th April when the 'Orry' was refloated on a high spring tide, and she returned to her berth under her own steam and with the assistance of the former Isle of Man harbour dredger *Mannin 2.*

The Steam Packet Company sent the *Mona's Queen* to Manchester for her annual overhaul and the 'Queen's' passage along the Ship Canal on 8th January aroused great interest.

The new *Lady of Mann* [2] ran her trials on the Clyde between 15th and 22nd June. She arrived in Douglas direct from Troon at 21.00 on 29th June, several weeks late. The Company had had to operate the T.T. Week sailings with just six vessels. The 'Lady' went straight into passenger service with her maiden voyage from Douglas to Liverpool on 30th June. She was a more powerful ship than the 'Queen', and did not suffer the teething troubles of the earlier vessel.

Car ferry sailings from Fleetwood were inaugurated by the *Mona's Queen* on 15th June 1976 but the response was less than enthusiastic: only 2,000 cars were conveyed on 88 sailings, an average of just 22 per crossing.

Despite the summer of 1976 being the hottest of the century, the Company reported a drop of 12,000 in the total number of passengers carried when compared to 1975.

1977

In mid January 1977, the Chairman of the Isle of Man Harbour Board announced that roll on – roll off facilities

Purser John Shepherd (left), Captain Ken Bridson (centre) and Piermaster Dennis Smith on the occasion of the *King Orry's* last voyage - Sunday 31st August 1975. *(John Shepherd collection)*

were being considered by his Board, but their provision depended on two major factors: (1) the building of a breakwater extension likely to cost around £5 million, and (2) the provision of a linkspan which might require another £2 million.

The construction of the new Liverpool Landing Stage still had problems. New stronger booms and reinforced land anchorages for the booms and bridges were being constructed after the original ones had failed in severe winter weather. In the event Steam Packet vessels first used the new stage in early July after the Royal Yacht *Britannia* had been alongside for some days during the Silver Jubilee Celebrations. The *Mona's Isle* represented the Steam Packet Company at the merchant shipping review on the Mersey on 21st June, when the Queen and the Duke of Edinburgh reviewed the assembled fleet from the decks of the Mersey ferry, *Royal Iris.*

The former cargo vessel *Fenella* [3], now trading as the *Vasso M* in the eastern Mediterranean, caught fire and foundered in May 1977.

Notwithstanding the statement from the Harbour Board in January, the Isle of Man Government agreed to expenditure of £650,000 to support the setting up of a ro-ro service, which would operate in direct competition with the Steam Packet Company. This sum would cover approximately half the cost of a linkspan installation in Douglas harbour.

In 1977 operating costs were higher than expected; for instance the annual fuel bill amounted to £1,270,000, six times the 1973 figure. With the threat of a new operator commencing on Isle of Man routes in 1978, it was decided to reduce the fleet to six ships. Subject to minor variations the full schedule of sailings could be carried out, although charter work might have to be curtailed.

Winter lay-up in the Morpeth Dock at Birkenhead with the ***King Orry*** for sale. *(John Shepherd collection)*

The *Lady of Mann* [2] leaving Douglas on her maiden voyage to Liverpool on 30th June 1976. *(W.S. Basnett)*

In November the *Snaefell* was offered for sale and was purchased by the Rochdale Metal Recovery Company. She had made her last sailing for the Company on Monday, 29th August. A year later, on 24th August 1978, the old steamer was towed to Blyth, Northumberland, for demolition.

The Steam Packet Directors made an exploratory trip from London to Zeebrugge and back on the Boeing Jetfoil operated by P&O to assess its potential for Manx routes.

In December 1977 the *King Orry* [4] was resold to Lynch & Son of Rochester and left Glasson Dock under tow of the tug *Afon Wen*. The 'Orry' arrived at Queenborough, Isle of Sheppey, on 21st December. Another long period of idleness now followed after she was towed to nearby Strood, and she was eventually broken up in 1979.

The *Snaefell* operated her last voyage for the Company in August 1977. She is seen here outside the *Mona's Isle* on the Victoria Pier. *(W.S. Basnett)*

From *Channel Entente* to *King Orry* [5]

The ***Channel Entente*** leaving Heysham for Douglas at Easter 1992.
(John Hendy)

The ***King Orry*** arriving at Douglas in August 1994. *(Miles Cowsill)*

CHAPTER 8
MANX LINE AND
THE MERGER
1978 – 1986

The 'Lady's' Silver Service Dining Room. *(W.S. Basnett)*

1978

The Manx Line was formed in 1978 by a group of Island businessmen, including former world champion motorcyclist Geoff Duke. The intention was that the new company, with its ability to carry lorries, would provide a long overdue roll on - roll off service to the Isle of Man, and stimulate a great deal more trade and industry on the Island. Coaches could also be carried, providing the opportunity for coach holidays from the mainland.

All the Steam Packet Company's car ferries had been specially built to load and unload from existing harbour facilities at Douglas, a system which had limited the size of vehicles carried to cars and light vans. By using Heysham as its UK port with its existing loading ramp, and a new 'MacGregor "F" type linkspan' at Douglas, Manx Line would overcome this problem. Items such as fertilizer and animal feed could be supplied in bulk and, for distribution purposes, chain stores could treat their Manx branches as if they were on the mainland.

The success of the bow thrust units installed in the two motor ships prompted the Company to have the *Ben-my-Chree* similarly fitted during her pre-season overhaul at Manchester. A unique steam powered bow thrust unit enabled the 'Ben' to be rostered for the Fleetwood service where it was necessary for the vessel to turn in her own length off the berth in the Wyre Channel.

It should be noted that in the case of the remaining 'classic' steamers *Mona's Isle* and *Manxman,* the practice was to swing the vessel at the Wyre light off Fleetwood and then proceed astern up the channel to the berth. The vessel was navigated from the flying bridge, from where the visibility was excellent. However in the case of the 'Maid' and the 'Ben', this visibility was not available from the wings of the bridge, and made this manoeuvre impractical.

On 23rd March 1978 the 2,753 ton motor vessel *Monte Castillo* of Bilbao arrived at Douglas and carried out berthing trials. The former Aznar Line vessel then sailed for Leith for a complete refit which included the fitting of a bow door. The Manx Line advertised its new Heysham to Douglas service to commence on 1st June.

The new company was accepting bookings up to late May when they suddenly announced that their service would not in fact be running before 1st July. The Steam Packet swiftly had to organise extra sailings at extremely short notice to carry the Manx Line T.T. traffic during the first ten days of June. Owing to industrial strife, the *Monte Castillo* (now renamed *Manx Viking*) did not leave Leith until 29th July, and arrived in Douglas for further berthing trials on 31st July.

In 1978 the Douglas to Dublin route was at last accepted by the Customs and Excise as a foreign one, and the Steam Packet Company were permitted to sell duty-free goods on board their vessels. With no suitable facilities available, two specially constructed trailers were purchased for use as duty-free shops, and these were driven on and off the Dublin bound vessel each voyage as required. The *Lady of Mann* was later equipped with a purpose-built duty-free shop.

On 15th August the *Lady of Mann* [2] crossed from Fleetwood to Douglas in a berth to berth time of 2 hours 39 mins, and the next day in 2 hours 40 mins. Despite being very fast passages they were still seventeen minutes slower than the *Viking's* record crossing in 1905.

The *Manx Viking* was finally granted her necessary certificates and the long awaited first official sailing of Manx Line's Heysham to Douglas link took place on 26th August 1978. On 8th September, only a fortnight after the service started, one of her diesel engines broke a piston, and sailings were again suspended. With the enormous loss of revenue as a result of starting the service so late in the season, plus the high cost of work carried out at Leith and Heysham, Manx Line was rapidly running into serious financial trouble. On 20th October came the announcement that Sealink and James Fisher had taken over. Fishers took up 490,000 of the 500,000 ordinary shares of Manx Line Limited, with an agreement that Sealink would take over later. In due course Sealink took up a 60% stake, leaving Fishers with the balance of 40%.

On the night of 1st December 1978, in the first severe easterly gale which had occurred since the installation of the Manx Line Victoria Pier linkspan, it broke adrift and severed its connection with the approach road, causing considerable damage to the Victoria Pier. Just under two years earlier, in January 1977, the Harbour Board chairman had said that a pre-requisite for siting a linkspan in Douglas Harbour was the construction of an extension to the Battery Pier breakwater to protect the harbour from easterly gales. In their haste to assist the new Manx Line, this advice had been ignored by the Government, and the result was plain for all to see on the morning of 2nd December.

Without the linkspan facility, the *Manx Viking* was unable to operate and was dispatched for major overhaul at the Belfast yard of Harland & Wolff on 12th December. There were many on the Isle of Man who considered the Manx Line operation finished.

Until the extension to the Battery Pier was built at Douglas, easterly gales would frequently see the Steam Packet vessels using Peel, on the island's west coast. There's snow on the hills as the **Ben-my-Chree** attempts to come alongside. *(W.S. Basnett)*

1979

The run of easterly gales continued throughout the winter of 1978 - 79, and the Steam Packet Company diverted their vessel to Peel on eighteen occasions - three times the normal winter average. The extra cost of diverting a vessel to Peel was upwards of £500 at 1979 prices. Foot passengers had to be bussed across to Peel, the practice being for the buses to leave the Sea Terminal at Douglas at 09.00, the advertised sailing time. The vessel would sail from Peel as soon as the passengers had boarded, and the passage to Liverpool took about five hours, depending on the severity of the easterly gale.

Conditions at Douglas could be very difficult in much less than gale force winds from an easterly point, and the breakwater extension scheme dated back to 1911. It was raised again in 1936 and also after the Second World War. In November 1979 the Isle of Man Government finally grasped the nettle and approved the expenditure of £7.2 million to protect and extend the Battery Pier.

In March 1979 the *Manxman* was chartered to a film company which was making yet another version of the *Titanic* disaster. The *Manxman* came out of winter dock and became the Cunard liner *Carpathia* in the film.

The steam powered bow thrust unit fitted to the *Ben-my-Chree* proved very successful and in the winter overhaul period, work was started on equipping the *Manx Maid* with a similar unit which was in use by the end of the summer season.

At the Steam Packet Company's 1979 Annual General Meeting the authorised share capital was increased from £1,500,000 to £3,000,000. (The amount the Company is able to borrow is restricted to three times the paid up capital.)

The *Manx Viking* arrived back on the Heysham - Douglas service in May 1979 using a temporary structure incorporating a bailey bridge erected at the north side of the King Edward VIII Pier at Douglas. The replacement linkspan finally arrived and was in place on the Victoria Pier in July when the full roll on -   roll off Manx Line service was restored.

1979 was Millenium Year in the Isle of Man, celebrating 1,000 years of the Island's Parliament, Tynwald. An extensive programme of events encouraged tourists to the Island, and the Steam Packet Company operated over 2,000 passenger sailings during the year.

1980

Monday, 30th June 1980 was the 150th anniversary of the launch of the Steam Packet Company's first vessel, the paddle steamer *Mona's Isle* [1]. Accordingly the *Mona's Isle* [5] was rostered to take a 'Round the Island' excursion. Unfortunately it was a dull day and only 333 enthusiasts were attracted. Earlier in the summer season, the 'Isle' had been used in the making of the award winning film, 'Chariots of Fire'.

The B&I Boeing Jetfoil *Cu-na-Mara* struck the *Manxman* as it was approaching the Liverpool landing stage on 2nd July. The *Manxman* was tied up alongside the stage and received negligible damage, whereas the Jetfoil was off service for a week!

Due to increased operating costs, the Company could no longer keep a reserve of vessels for summer only use and so the *Mona's Isle* was offered for sale at the end of the season. Her final passenger sailing was from Douglas to Llandudno on 27th August 1980 and the Liverpool to Llandudno excursion sailings ceased with her passing.

Despite speculation that the old steamer might be used as

The *SeaCat Isle of Man*

Top:- The SeaCat arriving at Douglas in August 1994. *(Miles Cowsill)*

Above and Right:- At speed off the Island, the SeaCat makes an impressive sight. *(both Island Photographic Co.)*

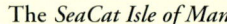

Left:- The *Mona's Isle* leaving Birkenhead for the breaker's yard in October 1980. *(John Collins)*

Below:- The operation of the opposition service from Heysham, with Sealink Manx Line's ro-ro ferry *Manx Viking*, eventually forced the Steam Packet into a merger. *(John Hendy)*

a floating restaurant on the Thames, the *Mona's Isle* was sold for scrap. The Beaumaris registered tug *Afon Las* arrived in Birkenhead to tow her away and at 14.30 on Thursday, 30th October she entered the Mersey for the last time bound for Dutch shipbreakers. The *Lady of Mann*, just in from Douglas, sounded a farewell salute as she slipped silently away in the afternoon sunshine.

In September 1980 the Steam Packet Company announced that they had placed a contract for the construction of a linkspan with O.Y. Navire AB of Finland. The unit would cost £1,500,000 and would be sited and the south side of the King Edward VIII Pier.

1981

The Navire linkspan was towed into Douglas on 2nd June 1981 and was ballasted in position on the south Edward Pier the next morning. To operate the new ro-ro freight service, the Steam Packet Company had chartered the pale blue-hulled *NF Jaguar* from P&O. This vessel had been built in 1971 as Silja Lines *Holmia*: she then became the *ASD Meteor* under the Singapore flag: then the *Penda* before becoming P&O Ferries' *NF Jaguar*.

The new ro-ro freight service was inaugurated on 19th June and the *Peveril* [3] and the *Conister* [2] were immediately made redundant. The 'old' *Peveril* made her final sailing from Douglas on 19th June and was immediately sold and renamed *Nadalena H*. The *Conister* had made her last sailing two days

earlier on 17th June and was sold for breaking up in Aviles, Spain, in November 1981.

1981 proved to be the Steam Packet Company's worst year of trading in its long history. After three very good summers, the number of staying visitors to the Isle of Man conveyed by the Company fell by 21.5% and the number of day-excursionists was down by 39%.

1982

In order to effect economies, the hulls of the four car-ferries were grit blasted down to bare steel, and then seven coats of self-polishing paint were applied to give a very

The Steam Packet's linkspan being assisted into position at the south Edward Pier by tugs of the Laxey Towing Company in June 1981. *(W.S. Basnett)*

The ro-ro cargo vessel *Peveril* [4] prior to being painted in Steam Packet livery. At this time she still sported the P&O pale blue hull colours. *(W.S. Basnett)*

smooth surface which, with the passage of time, would get even smoother and thereby reduce resistance. Sailing times were rescheduled and a computer supplied timings and courses which allowed for wind and tide.

The *Manxman* [2] was retained in the fleet for the 1982 season. She was now the very last 'classic' passenger steamer operating in British waters. However, in the generally depressed state of affairs it became clear that it was no longer economically possible to retain her, and she was offered for sale at the end of the season, at which time the Llandudno - Douglas sailings would also cease.

The *Manxman's* final passenger sailings took place on Saturday, 4th September and consisted of a Liverpool to Douglas day excursion advertised as 'Finished with Engines'. Just before departure from Douglas at 18.30 the weather

closed in with thick mist and drizzle descending on the Bay. Captain Peter Corrin backed the *Manxman* off No 4 berth on the Victoria Pier, and with her triple chime whistle sounding, she quickly disappeared into the mist. Just after arriving back at Liverpool at 22.40, Captain Corrin made a short speech over the tannoy and then, suddenly, it was all over: the end of a glorious era.

Marda (Squash) Limited of Preston bought the *Manxman* and she sailed under her own steam up the River Ribble to Preston on Sunday, 3rd October, carrying 1,000 passengers. At 12.48 she was alongside in the Albert Edward Dock - finally "Finished with Engines" after 27 years.

The *Hoofort* (ex *Ramsey*) was sold again, for trading in the Cape Verde Islands, and renamed *Boa Entrado*.

The high charter fees for the *NF Jaguar* were a major

In September 1982, the Steam Packet bade farewell to the 1955 built *Manxman* - its final 'classic' passenger vessel. She is seen here leaving Douglas for Llandudno, a month before the closure of the service. *(John Hendy)*

The *Manxman* [2] leaving Liverpool for static use at Preston on 3rd October 1982. *(John Shepherd)*

factor in the Steam Packet's ro-ro freight service not being viable. Consequently, towards the end of 1982, the Company exercised its option to purchase the vessel. James Fisher & Sons of Barrow effected the purchase, and chartered the *NF Jaguar* back to the Steam Packet Company on a long term bare boat basis on agreed demise charter terms which involved 120 payments totalling £2,293,783. The charter hire fees were effectively more than halved under this arrangement. The vessel was painted in Steam Packet colours, registered in the Isle of Man and renamed *Peveril* [4].

It was becoming evident in 1982 that the Manx tourist industry was in rapid decline. The number of staying visitors fell by another 8.7%, and day-excursionists were down by 6.9%. Equally evident was the fact that there was just not room for two passenger ship operators on Isle of Man routes.

1983

With the sale of the *Manxman*, the Steam Packet Company's passenger fleet was reduced to just the four car ferries. There was a further fall of 18,000 in the number of day-excursionists in 1983, despite generally excellent weather. Twenty-nine per cent of the Company's passenger traffic was on the Irish routes.

The Company returned to profitability in 1983 after the two loss making years of 1981 and 1982. Tenders were received for a new multi-purpose ro-ro vessel, but the lowest price quoted exceeded £20 million. Seen in this context, the year's profit of £351,857 was too low.

1984

The *Peveril's* cargo sailings in 1984 were disrupted almost constantly by a series of four strikes, and a total of 53 days' sailings were lost as a result of industrial action. On 9th July 1984, three of the Steam Packet Company's largest freight clients decided to transfer their cargo to the Sealink/Manx Line. The *Peveril* had the capacity to carry all the cargo requirements of the Isle of Man, but in effect the Company

was now carrying only 50% of that cargo. The freight service was once more plunged into a substantial loss-making situation.

The UK Government sold Sealink (of which Manx Line was a part) to Sea Containers Limited on 27th July 1984 as part of their privatisation programme. Sea Containers formed a wholly owned British subsidiary - British Ferries Limited, with a capital of £20 million, and which acquired the whole of the issued share capital of Sealink UK Limited.

The price of the heavy grade of fuel oil used by the two remaining steam turbine car-ferries *Manx Maid* and *Ben-my-Chree* increased by 30% during the year, a factor accelerating their withdrawal. There was to be no triumphant send-off for the last two steamers - the 'Maid' finished her summer season sailings on 9th September and retired to the Vittoria Dock at Birkenhead for lay-up, and the 'Ben' followed her on 17th September. It was announced at the end of October that both vessels would be offered for sale, despite there being considerable useful life left in both of them.

There was a further fall of 7.5% in the passenger traffic carried by the Company in 1984, despite another extremely good summer for weather. The number of day-excursionists was down from 126,000 in 1979 to 27,000 in 1984.

On 19th October 1984 the Steam Packet Company purchased the ro-ro vessel *Tamira*, formerly Townsend Thoresen's *Free Enterprise III*, for £600,000. The vessel was lying at Valletta, Malta, where she had arrived on 2nd September, having left Southampton on 24th August with a one-way consignment of British made motor vehicles for Malta on her vehicle deck. She had been purchased by George Zammitt and his Mira Shipping Company for this purpose, and was renamed *Tamira*.

Some work was carried out on the ship at Valletta and, under the command of Captain Vernon Kinley, she sailed for the Clyde on 7th December. On 8th November the Steam Packet Company signed an agreement with Burness, Corlett Limited, Naval Architects of Ramsey, in respect of professional advice in connection with part of the refurbishment of the ship which by now was renamed *Mona's Isle* [6].

The traditional two ship winter service finished at the end of December, with one vessel making the double crossing with effect from January 1985.

The Company reported an overall loss for 1984 of £245,244.

1985

The year opened with a veil of secrecy hanging over the Steam Packet's future operations after 31st March. No sailing schedules were published and no firm bookings were being taken, but it was obvious that the new *Mona's Isle* would not be sailing from Liverpool as there was no on-river linkspan

The **Ben-my-Chree** on the south Edward Pier while the Thoresen ferry **Viking III** is on the Manx Line linkspan relieving the **Manx Viking**. This picture dates from spring 1980. *(W.S. Basnett)*

there, nor were there any plans to provide one. It was also obvious that the Company was in severe financial difficulties. These stemmed from six years of competition from Manx Line, which at times had been charging wholly uneconomic fares. For much of the year there is barely enough passenger traffic on Isle of Man routes to support one operator, let alone two.

At 09.30 on the morning of 1st February 1985 a press conference was arranged at Imperial Buildings, the Company's head office. Speculation was rife that the Company was about to go into liquidation. In the event, a joint communique was issued from Sealink and the Steam Packet Company outlining a merger of their respective operations; the end of the Liverpool service and the concentration of the main year-round service on Heysham from 1st April.

The Chairman of the Steam Packet Company, Mr. S.R. Shimmin said on 14th March that the whole matter of the merger had become a most emotive issue, particularly on the Isle of Man, but it had to be judged in strict commercial terms. This emotion boiled over at a prolonged Extraordinary General Meeting held on 29th March which eventually approved the proposals for the merger with Manx Line. The proposals were to be implemented with effect from 1st April 1985 when the Company ceased its Liverpool operations. They included: (1) the allotment of 1,500,000 ordinary £1 stock units (40%) to Manx Line Limited - a subsidiary of Sealink UK Limited, and (2) an agreement that neither Sealink nor its subsidiaries would operate a ferry service to the Isle of Man so long as the Steam Packet Company used Heysham as its principal terminal in England. Sealink would provide the *Antrim Princess* on bareboat charter to operate the

main line service.

On the eve of the merger, 31st March, the situation was far from being auspicious. The Steam Packet Company's new flagship *Mona's Isle* was still at Govan with problems to her fire sprinkler system; the *Peveril* was strikebound in Liverpool; the *Antrim Princess* wasn't available, and the *Manx Viking's* survey certificates were due to expire within 24 hours. In addition the crew of the ro-ro vessel *Stena Sailor* were blockading the Heysham linkspan and refused to move as a protest about the *Peveril* replacing the Stena ship on the Belfast Freight Ferries run from 14th April.

A basic service was sailed by the sideloaders *Mona's Queen* and *Lady of Mann* until at 17.00 on 3rd April the *Mona's Isle* arrived in Douglas only to find that she would not fit either the Steam Packet's 'Navire' linkspan, nor Manx Line's 'MacGregor' linkspan. As the Heysham ramp was still blocked by the **Stena Sailor**, the 'Isle's' maiden voyage was on the Dublin route. On her arrival at Dun Laoghaire the problems

The **Mona's Isle** [6] (ex. **Free Enterprise III**) at Malta in December 1984. *(Captain Vernon Kinley)*

The *Mona's Isle* undergoing bow-modifications at Clydedock, Govan during January 1985. The extra steelwork was to cause serious problems with the vessel's deadweight. *(Joe McKendrick)*

of handling her in a stiff breeze became apparent: the bow thrust unit was inadequate and it was an hour before she was alongside. At one stage her engines had stuck in "full astern" mode inside the harbour!

Meanwhile, back at Birkenhead, the *Manx Maid* had been sold on 29th January to Devascus Limited. In February she entered the Bidston drydock for the removal of her fin stabilisers which were due to be fitted to the *Mona's Isle* which was equipped with the less effective flume stabilisers. On 10th April the 'Maid' left Birkenhead under tow for Bristol docks where it was intended that she should be used as a floating nightclub. On 5th February the *Ben-my-Chree* passed into the ownership of Mr. D. B. Mulholland. The plan was that she would become a restaurant ship in Jacksonville, Florida, and would cross the Atlantic under her own steam. A total of almost £300,000 was realised from the two sales a condition of which was that neither vessel should be re-employed on Isle of Man routes.

The Steam Packet abandoned Liverpool altogether after the final sailing by the *Mona's Queen* on 30th March.

On 19th April the Company announced that the *Mona's Isle* had serious deadweight problems and therefore could not carry anything like the loadings expected of her. A Liverpool firm of marine consultants, T.R. Little & Company, had surveyed the 'Isle' on 17th April and had established that the usable cargo deadweight amounted to 247 tonnes only. This problem had been caused by the extensive new accommodation built on the after passenger deck while this same new lounge area was also acting like a sail and making the 'Isle' unmanageable when berthing in a stiff breeze. To assist with berthing the Laxey Towing Company's *Primrose* and *Salisbury* were on stand-by at Douglas, and the *Carmel Head* of the Holyhead Towing Company was available at Heysham.

As T.T. week approached the Company found itself short of tonnage to meet the demands of the shuttle sailings for visiting motorcyclists, and so the *Ben-my-Chree* was chartered back from her new owners and registered in Liverpool. She sailed between Heysham and Douglas from 25th May until 9th June. Although laid up for eight months, the 'Ben's' brief return was a tribute to all the Steam Packet personnel who had achieved the impossible by returning her to service at just five days notice. Her unfailing reliability in a season which was lurching from crisis to crisis with the inadequate *Mona's Isle* was testimony to all those who had nurtured the Steam Packet's final steamer back to sea.

On Monday, 10th June the *Ben-my-Chree* left Heysham 'light ship' for Birkenhead and passed the Rock Light at 14.30

The *Mona's Isle* at the Edward Pier linkspan which she did not, initially fit. A new stern door was required after a brief period in service. Severe operational problems saw the vessel disposed of after just six months in service. (W.S. Basnett)

- the last steam powered sailing of all. The Jacksonville project fell through and for over four years the 'Ben' lay idle in the Vittoria Dock, sad and neglected.

The Steam Packet Company board meeting of 15th August resolved a number of outstanding problems. It was decided that the *Mona's Isle* would be permanently withdrawn on 5th October. Steam Packet Director Dr. E.C.B. Corlett had resigned on 24th June and the Board was now considering legal action in respect of the consultancy advice received from his Company over the *Mona's Isle*. The ship's replacement would be Sealink's *Antrim Princess* which would be crewed by Steam Packet personnel when she arrived in Douglas in the first week of October.

The *Antrim Princess* arrived at Douglas from Stranraer on 5th October and took up the schedules on the following day, joining the *Manx Viking*. The *Mona's Isle* was dispatched for laying up at Birkenhead on the morning of 7th October. Hers was the shortest of any career served by a Steam Packet vessel.

The *Antrim Princess* was renamed the *Tynwald* [6] and by the end of 1985 her port of registry had been changed from Stranraer to Douglas.

In 1984 the combined Liverpool and Heysham passenger carryings amounted to 197,000; whilst in 1985 just 170,000 were conveyed from Heysham, a decrease of 13.7%. Since 1979 holiday seasonal arrivals in the Isle of Man had fallen from 634,616 to 351,240, a decrease of 45%.

The Steam Packet Company's loss after taxation and extraordinary items in 1985 amounted to £3,047,941. Included in this figure is £1,657,384 being the loss incurred with the *Mona's Isle*, plus £386,000 for expenses, such as tugs, involved with operating the vessel.

1985 had been a year that the Steam Packet Company would wish to forget in a hurry!

1986

The Ardrossan sailings had been unprofitable in recent years and in 1986 a weekly summer seasonal service was substituted to Stranraer. The Company ceased operating scheduled services from Fleetwood, but Associated British Ports ran charter sailings from Fleetwood to Douglas on Tuesday and Wednesdays during July and August with the *Mona's Queen* marketed as the 'funboat'. A limited Liverpool seasonal service was reintroduced on Tuesdays and Saturdays using the *Lady of Mann*.

The *Mona's Isle* arriving at Birkenhead on 7th October 1985 at the end of her Steam Packet service. *(John Shepherd)*

The *Manx Maid* had been refused planning permission for the nightclub venture at Bristol, and on 8th February 1986 she left Avonmouth under tow of the tug *Indomitable* bound for Garston for breaking up.

On 14th March the Company concluded the sale of the *Mona's Isle* [6] at a gross sale price of $US 1,400,000. After conversion to £ sterling and after the deduction of sale related costs the nett proceeds were £710,502. The 'Isle' had been drydocked at Birkenhead on 21st February during which time she received an all white hull. The vessel was renamed *Al Fahad* and registered in Jeddah. Her new owners were Hassan Sadaka Hitta of Saudi Arabia who intended using her for trading in the Red Sea. The *Al Fahad* left the Mersey for the last time on 7th April, complete with two additional lifeboats which came from the *Manx Maid*.

The *Lady of Mann* appeared for the Easter sailings looking all the better for the complete absence of logos which had for the previous three years adorned all the Company's vessels. All the fleet were painted in Steam Packet livery, but the *Manx Viking's* funnels quickly reverted to the former Sealink colours of dark red with the 'three legs of Man' picked out in yellow. So much for integration!

A Douglas to Liverpool charter day-excursion took place on Saturday, 3rd May, the first Liverpool passenger sailings since 30th March 1985.

The *Peveril* completed her charter to Belfast Freight Ferries in mid-April and was then laid up in the Bidston

The *Mona's Queen* (with the *Stena Sailor*) at Stranraer on 25th May 1986 - the first day of the new service. *(M.J. Borrowdale)*

The chartered *Tynwald* [6] (ex. *Antrim Princess*) arriving at Douglas from Heysham in September 1988, with the *Lady of Mann* on the right. *(John Hendy)*

Dock. The Company announced that she would replace the *Manx Viking* in the Autumn. The carriage of hazardous cargo to the Isle of Man on the *Manx Viking* always created problems as it meant that no passengers could be carried, and it was therefore necessary to duplicate the sailings with a sideloader. The return of the freight only vessel eliminated this problem as well as reducing costs.

The *Manx Viking* operated the 11.30 Douglas to Heysham sailing on Monday, 29th September, and this proved to be her last sailing for the Steam Packet Company. After discharge she moved off the Heysham linkspan to a lay-by berth to allow a non Steam Packet vessel in. During the evening the N.U.S. threatened strike action over manning levels on the *Peveril* and the Company cancelled the 'Viking's' sailings for Tuesday, 30th September, fearing that the ship would not sail once she was loaded. The crew were instructed to take the 'Viking' to Birkenhead for lay-up, which they refused. Eventually she was laid up at Barrow

Members of the N.U.S. took industrial action on four occasions during the Autumn of 1986 which resulted in 58 sailings being lost. The *Tynwald* and the *Peveril* were both strikebound from Thursday, 4th December until Saturday, 13th December over manning levels on the *Peveril* - the longest disruption to services by strikes since 1966.

CHAPTER 9
RECENT TIMES
1987 - 1994

1987

The *Manx Viking* was drydocked on the Clyde in late February 1987 having been sold by Sealink to a Norwegian company for local services in the Stavanger area. She was renamed *Manx* for the voyage to Norway, and then sailed as the *Skudenes* on the Stavanger to Skudeneshaven run.

A return to happier Steam Packet days took place when the *Mona's Queen* operated a Heysham - Peel - Heysham charter sailing on Saturday, 4th July. In perfect weather and with 1,600 passengers on board, Captain Jack Ronan sailed the 'Queen' outwards to Peel via Langness and the Calf of Man, and returned to Heysham via the Point of Ayre and Maughold Head.

The *Manxman* was reported to be doing well at Preston Dock in 1987. Some 400,000 visitors had boarded the ship following her refurbishment to enjoy facilities which included 9 bars, 2 discos, a restaurant and a 'diner'.

The Company arranged to overhaul the *Mona's Queen* at Douglas in the Autumn and early Winter of 1987. She lay alongside the north Edward Pier and the new breakwater extension provided shelter from easterly gales. The last passenger vessel to 'winter' at Douglas was the *Victoria* in the early 1950s, although she lay at The Tongue in the inner harbour.

The passenger certificates for the *Lady of Mann* and the

Mona's Queen were reduced from 1,600 to 1,200.

The crew of the *Tynwald* went on indefinite strike on Tuesday, 29th December over the Company's proposals for revised pay and conditions. The *Tynwald* was at Heysham linkspan at the outset of the strike, and vehicles for the sailing to Douglas were trapped in the port for 47 days until the industrial action was called off on 13th February 1988.

1988

With the strike still continuing, the Steam Packet Company dismissed its 161 permanent ratings on 28th January 1988. The N.U.S. reacted and called a national ferry strike, which brought much of the U.K. ferry industry to a halt from 2nd February. The Company and the N.U.S. met at A.C.A.S. headquarters in London on Friday, 12th and Saturday, 13th February and reached a settlement with 114 men being offered their jobs back, and 47 being made redundant.

The *Tynwald* arrived in Douglas on Sunday, 14th February and normal sailings resumed on the following day.

During the afternoon of 29th April, members of the N.U.S. went on indefinite strike in support of striking P&O

The **Lady of Mann** and Liverpool waterfront. *(John Hendy)*

seamen at Dover. The *Tynwald* was at the Heysham linkspan and on the following day the port authorities cut her mooring lines so as to clear the span and the vessel was manoeuvred into the north berth at Heysham. The involvement of the *Tynwald's* crew in this dispute amounted to illegal secondary action and cost the union a great deal of money. In the event the action lasted until 13th May, with sailings being resumed on the 14th May.

In order to safeguard the T.T. race week traffic, the Isle of Man Government chartered the Skagerak ferry *Bolette* from

The **Mona's Queen** arriving at Douglas in stormy weather. *(W.S. Basnett)*

The *King Orry* and the *Lady of Mann* alongside at the Victoria Pier, Douglas. *(Island Photographic Co.)*

Fred Olsen Lines at a cost of £1 million for three weeks. With the strike over and the Steam Packet fleet operating normally, the *Bolette* was not required but nevertheless carried out a full programme of sailings. Holyhead was the principal U.K. port, but some Liverpool and Belfast sailings also took place. Loadings were light and on one sailing from Holyhead, just six passengers were on board. A 'Round the Island' excursion attracted almost 1,000 passengers.

Rumours abounded during the middle part of the year that a £7 million on-river linkspan was to be constructed at Liverpool on the site of the disused Waterloo river entrance. Sadly, this came to nothing.

The Manx Government commissioned a report from consultants which looked at all aspects of shipping services to the Isle of Man. It was published in May 1988 and was much criticised for its lack of understanding of the Manx trade. Most of the report's recommendations were rejected, but the Government resolved to dispose of their stockholding in the Company, and to acquire the two Steam Packet owned linkspans in Douglas harbour.

1989

The *Tynwald* was one of the ferries named by the Department of Transport as not meeting the latest 'stability in damaged condition' criteria.

During January 1989 the Company signed a contract with Wright & Beyer Limited of Birkenhead for a £2.6 million renovation of the *Lady of Mann*. The passenger accommodation was completely replanned and upgraded, and additional car space enabled her to carry an extra fifty vehicles. The 'Lady' returned to service on Friday, 26th May. Two days later she operated an evening cruise to the Calf of Man and Port Erin, actually turning to the landward of the ruined breakwater in Port Erin Bay. The 'Lady's' gross tonnage increased to 3,083 as a result of the rebuild, and her revised passenger certificate was for 1000.

The *Peveril's* starboard variable pitch propeller mechanism jammed in the reverse position as she was backing up to the 'Navire' linkspan at Douglas on Friday, 14th July. Extensive damage was caused to the ramp necessitating it being towed to Birkenhead for repairs by the tug *Waterloo* on Friday, 1st September. The *Peveril* did not suffer any structural damage as a result of the incident, but was sent to Harland & Wolff at Belfast for repair.

With both the *Peveril* and the *Tynwald* having to use the 'MacGregor' linkspan on the Victoria pier, much congestion resulted and the freighter's sailings were retimed.

After being laid up for 4 years, 2 months and 6 days, the *Ben-my-Chree* finally left Birkenhead for breaking at Santander on Wednesday, 16th August under tow of the tug *Hollygarth*.

After taking the Douglas to Fleetwood sailing on Wednesday, 30th August, the *Mona's Queen* left the Lancashire port early on 31st August and sailed directly to Cherbourg, arriving at 18.00 on Friday, 1st September. She had been chartered by the French post office, and sailed to the Solent to view the start of the Round the World Yacht Race in which their yacht *La Poste* was participating. On Sunday, 3rd September the 'Queen' was chartered by Sealink to deputise for their *Earl Granville* and sailed on the Portsmouth - Channel Islands route. After a further spell at Weymouth,

the charter terminated on 23rd September and the 'Queen' returned to Birkenhead.

On 24th August, the poorly supported seasonal service between Stranraer and Douglas was withdrawn. The repaired 'Navire' linkspan arrived back in Douglas after repairs on Thursday, 30th November and was immediately ballasted and replaced in position on the south Edward Pier.

Severe weather at the end of the year resulted in all sailings being cancelled on Christmas Eve. For the first time for many years, daylight sailings on Christmas Day were therefore operated by the *Tynwald* which left Douglas at 08.45 and returned from Heysham at 14.00.

1990

On 7th February 1990 the Steam Packet Company obtained approval from its stockholders to purchase the multi-purpose vessel *Channel Entente* (ex *Saint Eloi*) from Vessel Holdings Limited, a subsidiary company of Sea Containers Limited. The purchase price was $US7 million (£4.0 million). The ship had been built at Pietra Ligure, Italy, but although launched on 26th February 1972, the liquidation of her builders saw her seized by her creditors and laid up at nearby Genoa. Finally completed, the new train ferry arrived at her home port of Dunkerque on the first day of March 1975.

Captain Edward Fargher and a Steam Packet crew had brought the *Channel Entente* round from Dunkirk between 9th and 11th January 1990. She tested both the linkspans in Douglas harbour, and then berthing trials were carried out at all ports used by the Steam Packet Company. After the *Mona's Isle* fiasco, the Company was taking no chances! The *Channel Entente* was drydocked and then moved into the Bidston Dock, Birkenhead on Monday, 5th February. Her port of registry was changed from Dunkerque to Nassau prior to purchase by the Steam Packet.

As a part of the agreement to purchase the *Channel Entente*, Sealink UK Limited agreed to take back the *Tynwald* from the Company without penalty, although the charter still had some years to run. After arriving in Douglas on the morning of Monday, 19th February on her last Steam Packet sailing, the *Tynwald* sailed for Belfast at 11.00 for her end of charter drydocking, after which she went to the River Fal to lay up.

The *Channel Entente* arrived in Douglas on the evening of Saturday, 17th February, and on the next day was open for public inspection. Her maiden Steam Packet sailing on Monday, 19th February was delayed by severe weather and she left for Heysham at 12.20 instead of the scheduled 08.45. In extremely stormy conditions she immediately proved herself to be a good sea boat, in contrast to the very lively *Tynwald*.

On 22nd May 1990 an out of court settlement was reached between the Company and the third parties involved in the purchase and modification of the *Mona's Isle* [6], whereby the Steam Packet Company was paid £675,000 in return for its withdrawal of court proceedings against the third parties.

The *Tynwald* [6] was quickly sold to Agostino Lauro of Naples and sailed from Falmouth on Friday, 25th May for the Mediterranean under the name *Lauro Express*.

The future ownership of the Company was put in doubt

Arriving at Douglas for trials in February 1990 is the French multi-purpose ferry **Channel Entente**, (ex. **Saint Eloi**). (W.S. Basnett)

by a takeover bid launched in June 1990 on behalf of Sea Containers, who already owned 41% of the share capital. The bid of £1.15p per share was opposed by all the non-Sea Containers Directors on the board. On 17th July the House of Keys (the lower house of the Isle of Man Parliament, Tynwald) passed the first and second readings of the "Isle of Man Steam Packet (Regulation of Shares) Bill". This would, if enacted, have had the effect of preventing any stockholder not approved by the Isle of Man Treasury from holding more than 15% of the Company's stock, subject only to Sea Containers being allowed to retain, but not increasing, their 41% holding. On 2nd August, as a result of the Government's action, Sea Containers withdrew its bid for the Company.

The *Mona's Queen* covered the Liverpool sailings on Tuesday, 24th July and met with the Cunard flagship, *Queen Elizabeth 2*. After leaving the landing stage the *Mona's Queen* sailed down river to where the 'QE2' was anchored. In response to three long blasts on the *Mona's Queen's* syren, the 'QE2' replied with three long blasts of her own. The liner was at Liverpool to mark Cunard's 150th Anniversary.

The extra vehicle capacity on the shortly to be refurbished *Channel Entente* and the recently rebuilt *Lady of Mann* made the *Mona's Queen* redundant. Her passenger capacity was just not needed with the continuing decline of holiday visitors to the Isle of Man which in 1990 were 40% lower than in 1985. The 'Queen's' final sailing was the 08.00 from Douglas to Liverpool on Monday, 3rd September, but because of engine trouble this was able to convey cars only. After they had been

discharged the 'Queen' laid up in Birkenhead and has remained there ever since, despite various schemes being put forward for her future.

The *Channel Entente* was given a major refit at Birkenhead between 27th September and 4th December. A side door was cut into her hull to enable her to load vehicles at Liverpool meaning that she must always berth 'starboard side to' when using the landing stage. The vessel was back in Douglas on 6th December and after being open for inspection by shareholders, she was renamed *King Orry* [5] at a ceremony on Saturday, 8th December. The 'Orry' re-entered service with the 18.00 departure for Heysham on Sunday, 9th December, the event being marked with a firework display.

The SeaCat *Hoverspeed Great Britain* visited Douglas between Monday, 5th and Thursday, 8th November. On Tuesday, 6th November it made a non-landing round trip between Douglas and Heysham, taking 93 minutes on the outward run, and 90 minutes on the return.

The *Manxman* closed for business as a nightclub at Preston on 2nd June. Her berth was needed by developers at Preston Dock, and on the morning tide of Monday, 5th November she was towed down the Ribble estuary by the tug *Afon Las*. The tow was transferred to the *Brackengarth* at the Mersey Bar and the *Manxman* arrived in Liverpool's Waterloo Dock on Tuesday, 6th November. After some delay she re-opened for business as a nightclub and was marketed as the *Manxman Princess*.

The *King Orry* arriving at Liverpool by Robert Lloyd.

After purchase by the Steam Packet, the **Channel Entente** operated the 1990 season until she refitted at Birkenhead at the end of September and re-emerged as the **King Orry** [5]. She is seen leaving Heysham during April. (*John Hendy*)

1991

The Liverpool and Douglas winter service resumed after a five year gap on Saturday, 12th January 1991 when the *Lady of Mann* left Douglas at 08.30 in fine sunny weather. She left Liverpool on the return sailing at 18.30. The winter service operates on Saturdays only and is used by Manx residents wishing to spend a day watching football in Liverpool or visiting friends on Merseyside.

The new service rapidly gained popularity and the *King Orry* was fully booked on some Saturday mornings. The 'Orry' was crewed for 700 passengers which is normally adequate for the time of year, but from the beginning of March she was crewed for 900 passengers.

A Select Committee of the House of Keys (the lower house of the Manx Parliament) rejected the "Isle of Man Steam Packet Company Limited (Regulation of Shares) Bill" which sought to restrict ownership of the Company's shares. This left the door open for another possible take-over bid from Sea Containers.

1992

Recovery continued with pre-tax profits up 21% at £4.1 million. Passengers carried totalled 476,000 or 50.5% of all arrivals in the Isle of Man.

On 24th May the *Lady of Mann* operated a special Fleetwood to Douglas excursion to mark the 150th anniversary of the first such sailing by the wooden paddle steamer *Mona's Isle* [1] on 31st May 1842. In the course of the afternoon, the 'Lady' sailed on an excursion to Peel.

The summer schedules saw the introduction of 'through' services from Heysham or Liverpool to Belfast via Douglas, without changing vessel at Douglas. Meanwhile, the *Mona's Queen* was advertised for sale.

Whilst taking the 18.15 sailing from Liverpool to Douglas

on Saturday, 14th November the *King Orry* suffered a steering failure in the Queen's Channel at just after 19.00 and grounded on the Taylor's Bank about one and a quarter hours before low water. Hoylake lifeboat and the tugs *Bramley Moore* and *Hollygarth* went to the scene, and the 'Orry' was refloated on the rising tide at 22.30. She was towed back to Liverpool, where she arrived at 00.30 the following morning, and the Company made arrangements for the 374 passengers to be transferred to the Adelphi Hotel. The *Lady of Mann* was immediately brought back into service and restored passenger sailings with an 02.30 sailing from Liverpool on Monday, 16th November.

1993

The Steam Packet Company announced 'with regret' that it had been unable to agree terms with Sea Containers for the charter of a SeaCat. Had the SeaCat charter gone ahead, Sea Containers stated that they wished to transfer the *Lady of Mann* to the Victoria (British Columbia) to Seattle (Washington State, U.S.A.) service.

The Company's pre-tax profit for 1992 fell by 24% to £3.3 million. The continuing recession and reduced summer loadings were blamed. The freight vessel *Peveril* was purchased with a 'one-off' payment to James Fisher & Sons, terminating the demise charter.

The *Lady of Mann* commenced her summer season on Wednesday, 26th May with an eight hour cruise to take part in the review by Prince Philip (on board the Royal Yacht *Britannia* at Moelfre Bay, Anglesey) to commemorate the 50th Anniversary of the Battle of the Atlantic. Sadly, on the day of the Review a severe easterly gale was blowing and the 'Lady's' 492 passengers had a stormy passage.

On Wednesday, 2nd June, at about 16.10, the *Lady of Mann* was manoeuvring in Douglas harbour on arrival from

The rebuilt *Lady of Mann* re-entered service in May 1989. *(IOMSPCo./Island Photographic Co.)*

Liverpool, but instead of going astern into No 4 berth on the Victoria Pier, she surged ahead and collided with the Battery Pier. A temporary bulkhead was fitted forward of the bow thrust unit, and a temporary passenger certificate was issued.

The incident unfortunately happened at the height of the influx of visiting motorcyclists to the Isle of Man for the T.T. races, and a vast backlog of traffic built up at Liverpool. Some 200 motorcyclists were sent up to the Scottish ports of Gourock and Stranraer. Caledonian MacBrayne's *Pioneer* operated a single sailing from Gourock to Douglas and the *SeaCat Scotland* made a single Stranraer to Douglas trip in the early hours of Thursday, 3rd June. With temporary repairs carried out, the *Lady of Mann* was back in service with an 11.50 departure from Liverpool on Friday, 4th June.

Sea Containers purchased another 146,000 shares in the Steam Packet Company, bringing their total holding up to almost 42%. The Mannin Line, a wholly owned subsidiary of the Isle of Man Steam Packet Company, commenced operating a freight service between Great Yarmouth and Ijmuiden on Tuesday, 23rd November. The Company chartered Pandoro's *Belard* for the route.

1994

The usual winter overhaul arrangements took place with the *Lady of Mann* relieving the *King Orry* from 6th January until 5th February. The 'Orry' went to Cammell Laird's wet basin at Birkenhead rather than to the Bidston Dry Dock in the West Float. Further improvements to the passenger accommodation were carried out during this period off service.

The *King Orry* at sea after her total refurbishment during the autumn of 1990. *(IOMSPCo./Island Photographic Co.)*

The *King Orry*

Above:- The forward Summer Lounge.

Left:- The gift shop.

Below:- The King's Head bar.

(All photos: IOMSPCo./Island Photographic Co.)

Monarch of the Irish sea; the *King Orry* leaves Douglas on her daily run to Heysham. *(Rick Tomlinson)*

Douglas Harbour in late June 1994 with the **King Orry**, the **Lady of Mann** and the **SeaCat Isle of Man**. Beyond the 'Lady' can be seen the Caledonian MacBrayne vessel, **Claymore** which had commenced a weekly service from Ardrossan operating between May and September. *(Alan Watterson)*

On 11th March came the surprise news that a SeaCat was to be operated on Manx routes for the summer season and that on its entry into service, the *Lady of Mann* would be laid-up. The *SeaCat Boulogne* (from the Folkestone - Boulogne and Dover - Calais routes) was chartered from Sea Containers in late June. The Steam Packet Company stated that an 18 month charter of the fast craft had been negotiated and that the *Lady of Mann* would remain on stand-by until the end of the summer season. The Company's A.G.M. on 5th May turned into a somewhat prolonged affair with shareholders asking for assurances that the Company was confident of the success of the venture.

Some two years after closing for business as a nightclub in Liverpool's Waterloo Dock, the *Manxman* [2] left the Mersey for the final time at 14.00 on Saturday 16th April. The salvage tug *Freebooter* towed her to Hull where her owners, Midnite Entertainments, had plans for berthing her in a disused drydock and reopening her as a nightclub. Externally, despite her garish colours, the steamer is still recoginsable as the ship which the Steam Packet sold in 1982, but internally there is nothing left to remind the visitor that she was once the turbine steamer *Manxman*.

Visits to Peel are now rare. Here is the **Lady of Mann** during the last call in May 1992. *(Alan Watterson)*

Douglas Harbour from the north with the *Peveril* at the south Edward Pier ro-ro berth, the *King Orry* at the Victoria Pier linkspan and the *Lady of Mann* at berth 4. *(IOMSPCo./Island Photographic Co.)*

The Ardrossan - Douglas service reopened on an experimental basis on 28th May after a gap of nine years. It was operated in association with Caledonian MacBrayne using their vessel *Claymore*. A southbound sailing was operated on Saturdays with a return sailing on the following day. Passage time was eight hours and the service continued until the first week in September.

The T.T. race traffic was carried as usual by the *King Orry, Lady of Mann* and the *Peveril* but on Monday evening 27th June, the 'Lady' made her final passenger sailing with the 19.00 from Liverpool. The next morning at 08.00 she left Douglas 'light ship' for Birkenhead. Just like her namesake of 23 years earlier, she swept past the harbour entrance at Douglas sounding her whistle in farewell, with the *King Orry* in the harbour replying.

Meanwhile on 23rd June, the *SeaCat Boulogne*, by now renamed *SeaCat Isle of Man*, had arrived in Douglas from Liverpool where it had been handed over. The first passenger crossing was to Fleetwood on 28th June leaving Douglas at 10.00 and taking 94 minutes for the passage. On departure from Fleetwood, a mooring rope was sucked into one of her four waterjets and the craft missed the return sailing. The SeaCat was back in action on the following day leaving Douglas for Liverpool at 07.00 and taking 2 hours 20 minutes for the crossing. A £350,000 pontoon and ramp were provided at Liverpool to accommodate the craft.

The port of Heysham was closed on 12th July following an explosives find on a trailer in the port. The Company hastily arranged for the *King Orry* and the *Peveril* to be diverted to Fleetwood and even arranged for the pilot to be taken out to the incoming ships in a local fishing boat!

A long spell of calm and settled weather prevailed throughout July and August and it was not until 28th August that gales disrupted the SeaCat schedule. The Douglas to

Dublin departure was delayed 15 hours on that day and the Liverpool crossings were cancelled, passengers being diverted to and from Heysham on the *King Orry*.

During the summer months the SeaCat proved to be very popular with passengers and as a result of this, the seasonal sailings were extended to 26th September.

The success of the Mannin Line freight operation between Great Yarmouth and Ijmuiden prompted the Steam Packet to purchase the *Belard* (51 trailer capacity) on 15th August for £3.2 million. She was originally used on the Belfast - Ardrossan link (hence her strange name).

In August 1994, work started on the installation of the Manx Government's own linkspan on the north side of the Edward Pier at Douglas. Meanwhile at Liverpool, plans and feasibility studies for an on-river linkspan continued to be explored. The proposed terminal would be built on the Birkenhead side of the Mersey between the Woodside and Seacombe landing stages.

The *SeaCat Isle of Man* leaving Douglas. Her charter and entry into service in June saw the *Lady of Mann* retired for the rest of the 1994 season. *(IOMSPCo./Island Photographic Co.)*

CHAPTER 10
The Future

A shipping company can rarely create travel, rather it exists to meet the needs of people who wish to travel or to ship goods for a purpose. Its equipment must be chosen to meet these needs as efficiently and economically as possible, making best use of the technology available at the time. Over the history of the Steam Packet there have been many changes, from sail to steam to diesel, from loose cargo to containers to Ro-Ro, from travelling on foot to travelling with private vehicles. The Company has adapted to these changes, and has often been in the forefront. (Before the First World War the Steam Packet operated the two fastest ships around the British coast, and even today the *Lady of Mann* is the fastest conventional vessel on the west coast of Britain.) For passenger operation over distances such as those of the Steam Packet routes, fast craft operating at 35 knots or more average speed are emerging as standard equipment. We put a "toe in the water" in 1994, to great acclaim from many of our customers. Certain issues remain to be resolved - how to operate in the rough weather which is not uncommon on the Irish Sea and carriage of high vehicles such as coaches. It will be interesting to see whether twin or mono-hulls will prevail, whether diesel or gas turbine propulsion becomes the norm, and whether aluminium or steel hulls become standard for these craft.

For freight, the Ro-Ro mode is well established and seems likely to continue for the foreseeable future. Present speeds enable a reliable overnight service to be provided, which meets the needs of our customers.

It is a fast changing and challenging world, and the Steam Packet will be there among the leaders.

David Dixon
MANAGING DIRECTOR.

The *SeaCat Isle of Man* at the Liverpool Landing Stage in July 1994. *(Miles Cowsill)*

CHAPTER 11
Inside the Steam Packet

A DAY IN THE LIFE OF THE STEAM PACKET

Richard Kirkman. *(Miles Cowsill)*

Douglas 6.00am, Captain Jack Woods eases the *Peveril* stern first onto the South Edward Pier linkspan, a team of dockers wait ashore to tie up and discharge the vessel. At 6.12 the vessel is secured and voyage number 313 is completed. With a load of 37 unaccompanied trailers, 4 vans, a tractor and 13 trade cars to discharge, the dockers are soon reversing their distinctive orange tugmasters down the linkspan. Discharge is a slow process when the main deck has been emptied, as the upper deck can only be reached by using a lift.

Across the island businesses depend on the punctuality of the *Peveril* . At Marks & Spencer, Safeway and Shoprite stores, and at parcels depots, warehousemen await the arrival of their trailers with fresh goods packed the previous evening in giant warehouses in England.

For a short period, all the Steam Packet's operational fleet is together in Douglas Harbour. the *King Orry* is berthed at the seaward end of the Victoria Pier, whilst the *SeaCat Isle of Man* lies on the linkspan itself.

The *SeaCat's* 'B' crew boarded the craft at 6.00 in readiness for the morning departure to Liverpool. Following a briefing for the cabin crew - back at work after 2 days leave - loading commences at 6.35.

The ticket desk sales team and check in staff have been in place in their smart new office in the Sea Terminal since 6.00. At the check in desks bar coded tickets are checked within the reservations system and exchanged for computer printed boarding cards, and luggage is placed on conveyor belts and carried to the waiting baggage trolleys.

As passengers make their way into the SeaCat passenger accommodation they are greeted by the distinctively uniformed cabin crew, specially recruited for the season.

As departure time approaches, a final count of passengers and vehicles is taken from the reservations computer and the train of baggage trolleys is hauled onto the vessel. Assistant Traffic Manager John Harrison delivers the final tally to the vessel. With 424 passengers, 67 cars and 19 crew on board she is close to capacity. The crew complete their pre-sailing checks and, after the vessel has been made secure Captain Ken Crellin delivers a welcome over the vessel's public address system. Engines are started and, as the vessel leaves the linkspan on time at 07.00, passengers are called into the main lounge for a safety demonstration.

The *SeaCat Isle of Man* clears the harbour entrance and sets course for Liverpool. Within minutes she has reached a service speed of 35 knots and passengers settle down to enjoy the crossing. The Isle of Man is left behind in her wake and the advanced ride control system makes light work of the slight sea. In the Executive Suite, Customer Services Officer Philip Corrigan takes orders for breakfast.

On the *King Orry* the crew are a mixture of English and Manx based personnel. The former have slept aboard the vessel and the latter rejoin her in time for moving from No 2 berth onto the Victoria Pier linkspan. The manoeuvre takes around 9 minutes as Captain Edward Fargher (Commodore of the Steam Packet fleet) gently eases the vessel's stern onto the berth.

At 7.25, Colin Mather calls Manx Radio from the small 'studio' in the office and makes contact with disc jockey Stu Lowe in preparation for the morning SeaWatch broadcast. An exchange of banter precedes the more serious message about the day's sailing pattern. An advert for

day excursions from the island - prepared by Brunnings, the Company's advertising agency in Cheshire - concludes the broadcast.

At the Circus Beach holding area, the Check in staff begin issuing boarding cards to car passengers for the sailing to Heysham. Space on the Quay is cramped, and cars are soon marshalled on the roadway leading to the linkspan. The load is sufficient to justify use of the mezzanine car decks as well as the main deck. The *King Orry* loads and discharges only through the stern, and early arrivals drive their cars right round the car deck until they face the linkspan.

Foot passengers board through the new covered walkway, handing over their boarding cards immediately prior to boarding.

A much appreciated feature of departures from the Island is the sale of fresh kippers by Peter Hannah adjacent to the gangway. In the self service restaurant breakfast is proving popular, whilst elsewhere on the vessel the arrival of the morning newspapers creates a queue in the walk in shop.

This morning's car deck load is a mixture of cars, vans, bikes, coaches, and trailers and it is a skilled job to ensure that all are loaded safely whilst maintaining the vessel's trim. Loading is completed at 8.25 and Passenger Services Officer Malcolm Hill takes a reading of the ship's marks prior to departure. Once this information has been passed to the bridge and the ship made fully secure, Captain Fargher welcomes passengers on board and introduces a taped safety announcement and the vessel leaves the linkspan precisely at 8.30.

Operations Controller John Humphrey and Marine Superintendent Peter Corrin, having paid special attention to the punctual departure of the *King Orry*, walk from the ship through the Sea Terminal and across the road to the Head Office of the Company at Imperial Buildings where another working day is under way. Staff in telephone reservations have been taking calls since 7.00 and the workload is already beginning to rise as Travel Agents open for business. The early morning team are supplemented by additional staff as the morning progresses.

The *SeaCat Isle of Man* has made good time on her passage to Liverpool, passing the Bar at 8.47 and slowing for the last few miles up the River Mersey. As she makes her way up the river, the bridge observation deck is packed with passengers watching the crew undertake their duties. A purpose built pontoon has been added to the floating stage to allow loading and discharge from the SeaCat. Her arrival at the Landing Stage is 4 minutes early at 9.26 and discharge is rapidly completed.

Ashore the Liverpool Manager Tim Kerr and his team prepare for the 45 minutes turnround. Conditions on the Stage are cramped, as the facilities are temporary, awaiting redevelopment of the entire Princes Dock area. The best has been made of temporary Portacabin accommodation to provide a waiting area for passengers and a collection area for their luggage.

Departure is delayed by a large number of day excursion passengers

The *King Orry* arriving at Heysham from the Isle of Man. *(Miles Cowsill)*

arriving late for the sailing. The decision is made to hold the vessel and loading is not completed until 10.30. The load is again close to capacity at 430 passengers, 63 cars and 13 vans. The *SeaCat Isle of Man* is soon under way heading for the open sea.

On Board Services throughout the fleet are managed by Sutcliffe Catering. Sue Arnold of Sutcliffe is going through the accounts with Stephen Quirke (On Board Services Manager) and Mark Woodward, the Management Accountant. The accounts staff deal with all aspects of the financial transactions of the Company - from ticket sales to refunds. Much of the work is now computerised taking away a great deal of the routine figurework.

Dennis Duggan, the Public Relations Officer fields calls from the press about the success of the *SeaCat Isle of Man* and helps a wheelchair passenger with their travel requirements. His role encompasses many different aspects of customer relations and today is no exception in providing plentiful variety. Elsewhere Dave Morgan (Sales Manager - England & Wales) and Steve Taylor from Brunnings are discussing the autumn advertising schedule and taking a preliminary look at the 1995 brochure.

Personnel Officer Andy Kennish looks after crew on the *King Orry* - a request for leave to attend a funeral is dealt with sympathetically and cover arrangements are put in place.

Elsewhere in the building, the 'backroom' team are undertaking the day to day tasks essential to the smooth running of any successful organisation. From checking accounts to reconciling cash, preparing the wages to handling insurance claims, the range of functions is wide.

In the Board Room, Managing Director David Dixon and Passenger Manager Richard Kirkman join John Humphrey in a preliminary discussion about the 1995 timetable.

Not all Steam Packet activity is taking place on the Isle of Man. Sales Manager for Ireland and Scotland, Geoff Corkish is in Dublin meeting with the Company's Agent, Gerry O'Kelly, and Bill Walshe of the Marketing Division, the Company's Irish PR Agent. Their discussions range from the current advertising campaign in Ireland to the opportunities presented by press visits to the Island and new ideas for 1995. Geoff takes the opportunity to visit Chris Liddy of Isle of Man Holidays on Eden Quay to discuss his Autumn charter of the *King*

Orry from Dublin to the Isle of Man.

Fleet Engineer Mike Casey is travelling on the *Stena Sea Lynx II* between Holyhead and Dublin with design consultant Barry Finnegan of Portland Design, looking at ideas for the 1995 refit of *SeaCat Isle of Man* .

The *King Orry* has an uneventful passage and arrives in Heysham at 12.08 berthing stern to the No1 linkspan. The passenger gangway is soon in position and cars are simultaneously discharging over the stern ramp. Within 20 minutes the ship is empty and ready for her return load.

Passengers travelling onward by rail can normally catch a train direct from the quayside at Heysham but during the summer of 1994 the connection was replaced by a bus to Lancaster due to engineering works at Morecambe. Passenger Manager Eddie Ainsworth and his staff guide rail passengers across the forecourt to the waiting bus.

The *SeaCat Isle of Man* has made light work of the passage from Liverpool and completes her journey in just under 2 hours 30 minutes. Captain Crellin, assisted by First Officer Mick McGahan secure the vessel on the No1 linkspan in Douglas at 13.00 and discharge is completed within 9 minutes. The baggage train proceeds up the linkspan and round to the Sea Terminal where passengers collect their luggage from the newly installed carousel.

Day excursionists make their way ashore for a full afternoon in the Island. On the craft, refuelling takes place, ensuring that fuel tanks are kept topped up. Fresh supplies are taken on board to replenish stocks sold on the journey.

Car deck loading of the *King Orry* is completed at 14.05, with another mixed load of traffic demonstrating her flexibility in handling both freight and passenger traffic. The *King Orry* finally departs Heysham at 14.20 having been delayed slightly by the connecting rail/bus service. Passengers enjoy the wide range of facilities on board and the journey soon passes. The cinema is showing 'Philadelphia', the Children's Play Area is full of youngsters exhausting themselves, the Verandah Bar is doing a brisk trade, and in the Coffee Shop the afternoon tea is proving popular.

In the office of Magic Holidays, Colin Morgan controls the Company's Tour Operating subsidiary, offering a range of packages both to and from the Island. Charlie Henry looks after the specialist ATOP reservations system. Today Colin is beginning the preparatory work for the 1995 season by visiting a number of Hotels in Douglas to discuss their possible involvement. The TV advertising campaign has catalysed considerable interest in the Magic Holidays product and the phones are busy throughout the day with both queries and bookings.

Dixie Deane has special responsibility for developing new motor sport business for the Company and has been instrumental in developing the Jurby Race Circuit and Hill Climbs. Outside work he is Chairman of the Manx Motor Racing Club and works energetically to promote the Manx Classic.

Across in Fort Street, where the Company's subsidiary Fort Street Engineering Services have their workshops, the tradesmen combine their marine skills with a growing amount of outside business. They have learned new skills with the introduction and maintenance of the SeaCat service and are completing three portable gangways for a new operation in Qatar, due for shipment to the Gulf at the end of the season.

Quality Manager John Dagnall checks procedures with Fort Street Manager Charlie Coole - John has already successfully guided the Reservations, Marketing and Shore Operations functions to BS ISO EN 9002 (1994) accreditation and is now compiling documentation in readiness for appraisal of the engineering operation later in the year.

Masters change over on a Wednesday on the *Peveril* and Captain Steven Cowin has replaced Captain Duggan. Departure of the *Peveril* is some five minutes late at 16.35, but she is soon passing Douglas Head and setting course for Heysham with a load of 25 trailers.

The crews have also changed over on the *SeaCat Isle of Man*. Captain John Attwood and First Officer Dermot O' Toole prepare for the 17.30 departure for Liverpool. The Liverpool sailings have proved extremely popular and another full load is in prospect. It has been a sunny afternoon on the Island, and day trippers are reluctant to leave, but eventually all are on board. A punctual departure is essential as the *King Orry* is due on the berth soon after the the *SeaCat Isle of Man* has departed.

The *King Orry* arrives at Douglas Head at 17.50, passes through the pier heads and reverses onto the No 1 linkspan, docking on time nine minutes later. Her load is fully discharged within 25 minutes and she is soon ready to shift to the No 2 berth on the Victoria Pier. releasing the linkspan for the later arrival of the *SeaCat Isle of Man*. The crew complete their cleaning duties and stand down at 19.00.

On Board Services Manager Stephen Quirke meets with his shipboard team to discuss the week's performance. Thursday is crew changeover day on the *King Orry* and there are a number of issues to discuss as it will be another week before this watch reassembles.

Meanwhile, the *SeaCat Isle of Man* arrives at the Liverpool Landing Stage at 19.56, a few minutes ahead of schedule. Deputy Marine Superintendent Vernon Kinley has acted as pilot up the River Mersey. Speed on the crossing averaged 34 knots.

Day excursionists from the Isle of Man - a completely new market in 1994 - have enjoyed a full day on Merseyside. Businessmen have also taken advantage of the freedom which an extended day with their car gives them. The return departure time of 20.45 gives each the opportunity to make the most of their day.

Loading is completed at 20.44 and the *SeaCat Isle of Man* heads back for the Isle of Man. As she reaches the open sea and her full service speed, a message is received from Liverpool Coastguard to proceed to assist a fishing vessel on which a crew member has been taken ill. Captain Attwood steers a new course, but a further call advises that a helicopter has arrived at the casualty position and that *SeaCat Isle of Man* can stand down and resume her original course.

The 'twilight shift' in reservations at Imperial Buildings finishes at 21.00 and the last clerical staff make their way homeward.

Meanwhile the *Peveril* has made good time on her passage to Heysham and on arrival in the port has to wait some 7 minutes alongside the North Quay for her berth to become free. Turning round in the harbour, she reverses onto the No 2 linkspan and is secured by 21.16. Discharge commences soon thereafter.

The *SeaCat Isle of Man* arrives back on the Douglas linkspan at 23.19 - just 4 minutes late after her deviation on passage. Discharge is fully completed at 23.35, and whilst the cabin crew continue their cleaning duties on board, Captain Attwood shifts the ship past the *King Orry* and onto the No 4 berth on the north side of the Victoria Pier in readiness for the morning departure to Dublin.

The *Peveril*'s 01.00 departure time is crucial for businesses on the Island such as Marks & Spencer. A balance has to be achieved between leaving the central warehouse at Crewe as late as possible - thereby loading with the widest range of fresh produce - and arriving in the Island in sufficient time to have these products in the store for opening at 9.00 the following morning. The reliability of the overnight sailing allows businesses to keep stock levels low, secure in the knowledge that only extreme weather conditions will disrupt deliveries. A punctual departure from Heysham ensures a right time arrival in Douglas and prevents delay to other operators in the Port.

Captain Cowin guides the *Peveril* out of Heysham Port and sets course for Douglas. Another day in the long and illustrious history of the Steam Packet is about to begin.

Richard Kirkman

A Saturday afternoon scene at Douglas in August 1994, with the *Claymore* and *SeaCat Isle of Man*. (Miles Cowsill)

Above:- The port of Heysham with the *King Orry* and *Peveril* at the linkspans. *(Sea Containers Ltd)*
Below:- The new Sea Terminal at Douglas, (Inset) An Edwardian view of the terminal at Douglas. *(Miles Cowsill/Manx Museum)*

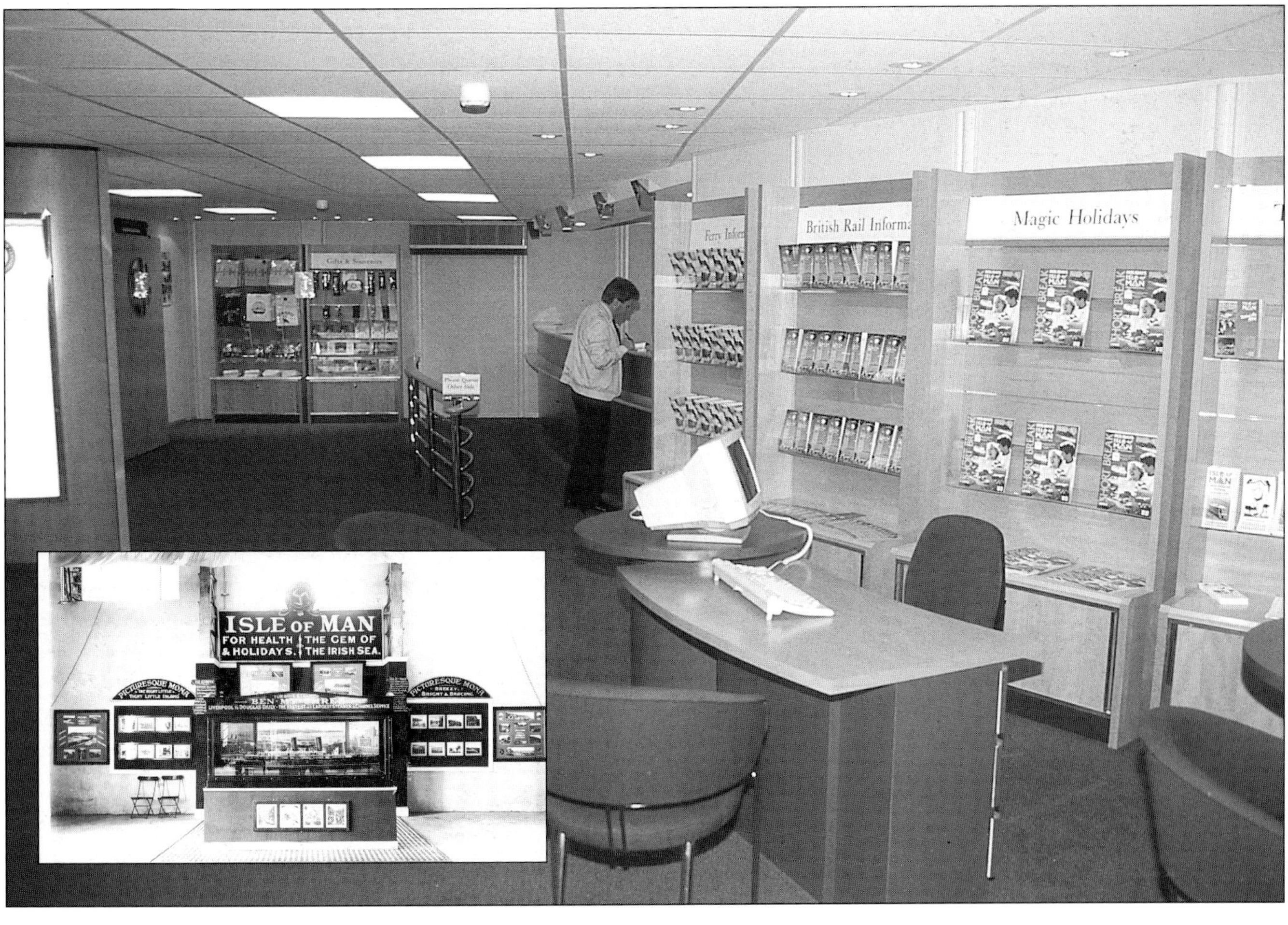

A MASTER'S VIEWPOINT

My sea-going career started by way of one of the traditional routes. After some time in a local fishing boat I joined my first ship, the Ramsey Steamship Company's *J. B. Kee*. She was a small coal burning coaster – 107.5 feet long with a gross tonnage of 241 tons.

The next few years saw me in the Zillah Shipping Company and Coast Lines. In 1954 I joined the Isle of Man Steam Packet Company for the first time as AB on the steam ship *Conister*, serving with the late Captain Griffin who at that time was on his first command with the Company. At the end of the summer season I went into Foreign Going ships, the first of which was the *Sulima* belonging to Elder Dempster. I had a enjoyable 10 months on a voyage to West Africa which included a round trip from the West Coast to North America.

At this time I was registered on the Liverpool "Pool". This was the Liverpool branch office of the British Shipping Federation. This organisation brought ships and crews together. Seafarers were offered a contract and became "Established", this guaranteed employment on vessels registered with the Shipping Federation and effectively replaced the casual labour aspect of seafaring.

Life on the "Pool" at the time was very varied and you could virtually pick any type of ship and sail to almost any port in the world.

By now I had realised that my education had to be completed if I was to further my chosen career at sea. After completing the required sea-time, that is an aggregate of time actually spent on board a sea-going ship and amounting to a total of four years, I enrolled at the Liverpool Nautical College then sharing premises with the College of Building in Clarence Street. The "Second Mate's" Class at the time was presided over by Captain Nelson and it is mainly due to his efforts that I emerged some time later from the Department of Transport examination room at Orleans House, Liverpool the proud possessor of a brand new Second Mate's Certificate. I joined Furness Withy and Company as a navigating Officer trading to the West Coast of North America via the Panama Canal until it was time to return to the College for the First Mate's course and examinations. The College was now part of the Liverpool Polytechnic in Byron Street.

After "First Mate" I served on the Furness Withy iron ore carriers: this was very much like my early days in the coastal trade. The ships were chartered to the British Iron and Steel Corporation and after discharge at one of the UK steel works could be sent out to any of the world's ore ports for a cargo. After about six months in this trade I joined the Cunard Steam Ship Company and spent several years sailing on all the Cunard routes, mainly North America, Gulf of Mexico and the Mediterranean. In the meantime I again returned to Liverpool to take my Master's Certificate.

In 1964 I returned to the Isle of Man Steam Packet Company. My first job was as Second Officer in the *Manxman* with Captain Ernest McMeiken. Promotion was quite rapid around this time and I soon found myself Chief Officer of the *Fenella*. In March 1976, after serving as Chief Officer in all of the Company's vessels except the *Lady of*

Captain Vernon Kinley *(W.S.Basnett)*

Mann, I was given command of the motor vessel *Conister*. The *Conister* along with the *Peveril* maintained the Company's container service to Liverpool. This service operated from the Hornby Dock in Liverpool to the Office Berth at Douglas for five nights from Monday to Friday with the option of Saturday and Sunday nights if required.

The inward vessel would lock out into the River Mersey when the dockers had finished at 17.00 hours and would arrive at Douglas, generally before midnight. The Office Berth was in the inner harbour and dried out at low water and could only be reached by *Peveril* and *Conister* about two and a half hours before and after high water. This usually meant shifting into the berth sometime during the night for an 08.00 hours start. The outward vessel would leave as soon as the tide would permit and arrive at the Hornby Dock Liverpool for an 08.00 hours start. This service ran very successfully until it was replaced by the new *Peveril* and the Ro-Ro service.

My first passenger vessel command was *Manxman* joining her in Liverpool, relieving Captain Ken Bridson. I remember being outward bound in the Mersey Channel in fog and catching a brief glimpse of the inbound *Conister* with Captain Corrin on board doing his first trip as Master.

In common with other ferry companies, the Steam Packet Masters hold pilot's Licences for all the ports on the regular routes. This means that they are expected to have a detailed knowledge and good experience of the port and approach channels. A designated number of trips have to be made into and out of the port with a licensed Pilot or Master on board. After this qualifying requirement an examination is conducted by the Harbour Authorities and only after they are satisfied as to the competence and depth of local knowledge attained by the candidate is a Pilotage Certificate issued. This certificate is renewed every year after satisfying the Harbour Authorities that the requirements and standards are

The **Ben-my-Chree** pictured on passage to Douglas. *(Captain Vernon Kinley)*

continuing to be met.

Each port and channel has its own peculiarities and every entry and departure demands a different approach and technique, and the variable aspects of the port have to be considered before making an approach. Probably the first consideration is the state of the tide. If, for example, the tide is at the lowest level and the underkeel clearance is reduced, the ship tends to 'smell' the bottom which can dramatically alter her handling characteristics. On the other hand a certain amount of shelter from the effects of the wind can be gained due to being low down relative to breakwater and piers once the ship is inside the harbour. At high water the reverse can occur in that the ship's handling characteristics can be restored, but shelter from the pier lost. The tidal stream varies continuously in rate and direction as the tide ebbs and flows and moves from springs to neaps. Tidal steams can change direction very quickly as some bank or other feature covers or uncovers with the rise or fall of the tide.

The weather condition at the port plays a large part in any manoeuvre and in cases of severe weather conditions, including bad visibility, a Captain has to very carefully consider all aspects and variables and decide if a safe entry and berthing is practicable. This pinpoints the solitary nature of the Captain's position because having considered everything, including any advice, the responsibility rests firmly with him and if things do not go well there will be 'experts' aplenty to criticise and apportion blame.

I think I can speak for my colleagues who were in the *Manxman, Mona's Isle* class of steamers when I say we would not have missed the experience. Handling the steam turbine ships without the assistance of bow thrusters and twin rudders called for a great deal of team work. The Second Officers took the wheel on the approach to the harbour and, working closely with and under the direction of the Captain, steered the ship to the berth. The Chief Officer and his team forward made sure a line was passed ashore as soon as possible: this was vital, particularly in poor weather. Aft, the seaman in charge would get his line ashore making sure the propellers were clear.

What was not so obvious of course was the activity below in the Engine and Boiler Room. The Chief Engineer was personally in charge on the manoeuvring platform and kept an eagle eye on the telegraphs and engine movements. It has been said that the Chief Engineer knew how a particular Captain manoeuvred the ship and sometimes knew what engine movement was coming before the Captain rang the telegraph. Probably there was a certain amount of truth in this! The Boiler Room was under the control of the Second Engineer who along with his team skillfully produced the steam to drive everything as and when required. I have always had the greatest of respect for my colleagues 'below' and hope the question 'what the hell is he doing up there now?' was not heard too often.

The introduction of the variable pitch propeller, twin rudders and bow thrust has been a big step forward. However, ships have got bigger, the ports stay the same size and more is expected from the ships. 1994 saw the introduction of Fast Ferries to the Island in the form of the Passenger Car Catamaran *SeaCat Isle of Man* and we are now learning new skills.

In 1987 the Managing Director Mr David Dixon asked me to take the position of Deputy Marine Superintendent. I was very pleased to accept as this meant working closely with Captain Peter Corrin, the Marine Superintendent, and still be able to spend time at sea on the ships.

Being in the Steam Packet gives a sense of sharing the

The *Lady of Mann* at sea. *(John Hendy)*

experience and tradition gained from over one hundred and sixty years of operation. When you consider that the Company started running ships only 25 years after Trafalgar, 15 years after Waterloo and 46 years before the Battle of the Little Bighorn and is still running ships today, this is something to be proud of.

Captain Vernon Kinley

THE ROLE OF MARINE SUPERINTENDENT

The title of Marine Superintendent is arguably the oldest within the Company. Although the title may not have changed over the years, the role in many respects has and probably never more so than in the last few years. After serving in all the Company's vessels as Master since 1978 it was a great privilege to be appointed to the position following the untimely death of Captain Harvey Collister in the summer of 1987. That was also shortly after the tragic accident involving the *Herald of Free Enterprise* which was to project ferry travel in general and Marine Safety matters in particular into the sharp focus of publicity. To some extent it has remained there ever since and the public are now much more discerning on such matters.

The most important facet of the role of Marine Superintendent is that of the operational safety of the Company's vessels. It begins with ensuring that vessels meet all their statutory requirements and have been issued with necessary certificates and documentation required for their operating areas. Not only though is it important for the vessels to be structurally and mechanically sound but of course they must be operated by qualified, experienced and competent personnel. Direct operational responsibility lies with the Master and his crew but to enable them to function effectively requires support and guidance from ashore. Although this is something which we have done for many years, it is now reinforced by the legal requirement for there to be a Designated Person appointed ashore. This quite naturally comes under the brief of the Marine Superintendent.

Operational safety covers a wide range of activities but principally concerns the safe navigation of the vessel and that equipment is provided and maintained for that purpose. Even though we hope we never have an emergency situation to deal with, it is nevertheless vitally important that the vessels are

The *Mona's Queen* on passage to Belfast. *(Captain Vernon Kinley)*

equipped and personnel are trained to deal with one. Therefore it is necessary to monitor proper on-board emergency procedures including regular and realistic drills. Encompassed within this is planning to protect the environment and contingency planning in general.

Effective safe management needs to be a two way process and it is vital to maintain good channels of communication between ship and shore. To achieve this we have in each ship a Co-ordinating Master, with whom I have regular liaison on all aspects of the ship operation. All our procedures are monitored and audited internally as well as being checked from time to time by the relevant Marine Authorities and independent auditors.

Another part of my remit is to the promulgation and monitoring of all matters relating to Occupational Health & Safety. This deals with matters of safety for passengers and crew in terms of health and welfare as opposed to navigational and operational matters. This is embodied by the appointment on each vessel of a Safety Committee under the chairmanship of the Master. This committee meets at regular intervals and any matters raised are reported to my office from which they are considered and discussed with my management colleagues.

This is equally the case for many other facets of the job. Although each member of the management team has individual and well defined areas of responsibility, nevertheless it is vital there is a dovetailing of all of those responsibilities through teamwork. For any Company, the image it projects is very important and the Steam Packet is no exception. Part of that is ensuring so far as practicable that the cosmetic appearance of the vessels is maintained to a high standard. They are completely painted at overhaul but thereafter it is necessary to arrange and supervise the required schedule for the maintenance of the standard with their respective ship's officers and crews.

One of the most interesting tasks I have to perform is advising the Board on all matters marine. This is particularly so in the acquisition of new tonnage. It is likely to mean inspecting and perhaps sailing on the subject vessel and thereafter advising the Board through the Managing Director.

In conjunction with this it may also be necessary from time to time to assess the feasibility of other routes and ports from a marine aspect. This was typified in the period prior to the introduction of the *Belard* on the Great Yarmouth/Ijmuiden route which was a geographical extension of the Company's interests.

The job is very diverse in addition the aforementioned safety considerations. It can range from organising the scattering of ashes at sea to the lending of a gangway net from which a charitable organisation may launch balloons.

It would of course be impossible to achieve any objectives without the assistance and support of a committed Board of Directors who consider safety to be paramount. I have the invaluable assistance and co-operation from colleagues in general and particularly that of my deputy, Captain Vernon Kinley and our Secretary Karen Cromwell.

On the vessels, through the Co-ordinating Masters and Chief Engineers, I am afforded the greatest assistance and co-operation from all the officers and crews and feel privileged to head a team of such skillful seamen and technicians.

This year has seen the introduction of a fast craft on our

Captain Peter Corrin *(Miles Cowsill)*

routes for the first time and with it there has been a need to revise some procedures and working practices. It could be said that the same applies to the role of Marine Superintendent. Although the title is long standing there can be no short sighted approach to the future when we will aim to match the oldest traditions with the newest technology and maintain the standards of safety and seamanship synonymous with the Company.

Captain Peter Corrin

THE STEAM PACKET IN IRELAND

Belfast

W. E. Williames, a name synonymous with the Isle of Man for many years, had been founded in 1870 by a well respected businessman of the same name. From the early years of his business, he had secured the agency for the Isle of Man Steam Packet Company and sold passages to the island as well as emigrant passages to the new worlds of America and Australia. In those days shipping lines and their agents provided travel as an extra to their freighting business and Williames was no exception. He built up a respectable freight business both in coastal waters and further afield.

Not a lot is known about Mr. Williames except that he was a confirmed bachelor, who loved cats. Legend has it that as many as thirty cats were allowed to roam the offices. In those days the offices were in the heart of the docks so perhaps the cats were there for more than their owner's pleasure.

The business continued to flourish under Mr. Williames' guidance until 1910 when the company was sold to two gentlemen, Messrs Stephens and Walkington, who had set up

The *Lady of Mann* arriving at Dublin. (IOMSP C0)

in business as timber brokers. Mr. Walkington was killed during the First World War. The ownership then passed to the Stephens family who retained the same until 1981. Ownership then passed to the George Bell Group of Dublin. A management buy-out took the company back to local ownership in 1987.

Today W. E. Williames continues to work as Agent for the Isle of Man Steam Packet Company Limited, operating from two locations in Belfast. The main office is on Nothern Road, inside the harbour estate. Here staff are on hand to take enquiries or make bookings etc. In the summertime a bureau is opened in the passenger terminal on Donegall Quay. Again, enquiries and bookings can be made at this bureau. Personal callers are welcome at both locations.

Working for the Isle of Man Steam Packet Company Limited is more than just an Agency for passenger tickets. Williames is involved in all aspects of marketing the service in Northern Ireland, and each season makes a contribution towards planning for the next.

On the operational side of the business, Williames has provided husbandry services to the ships in Belfast when drydocking, superintendence for disembarking and embarking passengers and cars etc.

At the end of the 1991 season, it was evident that the berth the Company had been using for many years had reached the end of its useful life. The port authority allocated part of the passenger terminal area on Donegall Quay. This terminal is much more accessible for travellers. However, the gangway accesses from the passenger walkways were not compatible with the ships, the linkspan was not suitable for the *King Orry's* stern door and the side loading ramp for *Lady of Mann* could not span the gap between the quay edge and the ship.

Quite a project was put in hand which Williames co-ordinated. By Easter of 1992 the berth was capable of handling the *King Orry* and by the time the season properly commenced, the Company was operating from a terminal which could accommodate any of their ships and embark passengers without them being exposed to weather.

The terminal building has been refurbished and travellers are afforded a comfortable departure lounge with snacks and light refreshments, television and a children's play area.

In 1994, when the *SeaCat Isle of Man* was introduced, Belfast was fortunate enough to have a berth on the terminal specifically designed to handle such craft.

The SeaCat service has had a very positive effect on

carryings out of Belfast and it is hoped that this, allied to the peace dividend in Northern Ireland, will see growth continue and perhaps even create a new market for Manx residents to visit Northern Ireland. It would be a lovely sight to once again see a queue of people wanting to buy tickets for the Isle of Man.

John McArthur

Dublin

Dublin Maritime Limited were appointed as general sales agents for the Isle of Man Steam Packet Company in February 1989. At that time the service operated from a small terminal on North Wall Quay.

In October 1993 the Isle of Man Steam Packet service transferred from North Wall Quay to Dublin Ferryport where it now shares the use of a new Sea Terminal at Berth 43 with B&I Line. 1995 sees plans for the improvement of this terminal to include additional facilities for passengers including baggage handling etc. This work is expected to be completed by June 1995.

Dublin Maritime represent the Isle of Man Steam Packet Company on the Ferry Users' Forum which was set up by the Irish Government to promote safety and facilities for passengers on board ferries.

The Isle of Man Steam Packet Company is also represented on the National Ferry Safety Committee which is affiliated to the International Maritime Organisation and covers all aspects of ferry safety.

The Isle of Man Steam Packet service is managed by Gerard O'Kelly based on North Wall, Dublin with reservations handled by Ms. Tracy Quinlan. A dedicated telephone line is available at Maritime House for travel agents.

In addition to the normal May-September schedules for Isle of Man Steam Packet, the vessel *Lady of Mann* was chartered for a sequence to be included in the film 'The Commitments' and the *King Orry* is chartered by Isle of Man Holidays (Dublin) each October for a bank holiday extravanganza on the Island.

Gerard O'Kelly

ENGINEERING DEPARTMENT

The ships of the Steam Packet, as the name implies, were originally driven by steam engines, a form of propulsion which was to serve the Company for well over 150 years. Paddle engines, steam reciprocating engines and steam turbines, ranging from the early direct driven to the latest geared type, all played their part in maintaining a reliable lifeline to the Island.

The first vessel with diesel engine driven main propulsion was the cargo vessel *Fenella* which appeared in 1951, although diesel engines had been used for many years for auxiliary purposes. Steam turbines were to remain the mainstay of passenger ship propulsion for the first two car ferries until the arrival of the diesel powered car ferry *Mona's Queen* in 1972. All subsequent vessels have been similarly powered including our current passenger and ro-ro vessel, *King Orry*.

The summer of 1994 was to provide a major change in

technology when the *SeaCat Isle of Man* came into service. She is powered by four water jets driven by diesel engines. Each jet pumps 11 tonnes of water per second producing about twice the horse power of the conventional ferries when pushing the vessel through the water at up to 38 knots.

The *SeaCat Isle of Man* has also been fitted with an additional piece of equipment known as a 'ride control system.' This is a form of stabilising device which consists of an inverted 'T' foil placed under the forward end of each hull with a trim tab fitted below each set of jets at the after end.

Both foil and trim tabs are hinged and are moved via hydraulics. Inside the vessel are accelerometers and gyroscopes which sense the craft's motion and move both foils and tabs to counter any movement as required. This helps to dampen high accelerations which have been known to make passengers uncomfortable.

Our ships and their machinery have, of course, to be looked after by engineers who throughout the Company's history have performed watch-keeping duties, maintenance and repairs on very different kinds of machinery - particularly over the last few years.

The main task of today's engineers on board the vessels is to run and watch-keep the main and auxiliary machinery. Short term maintenance and repairs are carried out by ships' engineers along with repairs to deck machinery and passenger services equipment.

Chief Engineers do not keep regular sea-going watches but are required to take charge of the engine control on entering or leaving port and whilst the vessel is within the confines of harbour, navigable channel or river. The other duties extend to considerable paper work in recording, monitoring and planning maintenance which enables major problems to be kept to a minimum. Once the vessel is 'at sea', the senior watch-keeper will either be a second or third engineer.

One engineer must remain in the control room at all times to monitor the instrumentation and make adjustments where required. Another engineer carries out an inspection of all machinery and machinery spaces once the vessel has left port and at regular intervals throughout his watch.

The bunkering (or refuelling) of the ship can be done from barge or road tanker. Depending on the quantity required, up to 100 tonnes can be taken from a barge which can supply heavy fuel oil for the main engines or marine fuel for the generators. Top-ups of about 20 tonnes can be obtained from road tankers.

The advent of the SeaCat operations in June 1994 brought new working patterns. The Chief Engineer is now a watch-keeper and is stationed in the wheelhouse sitting at a console monitoring all machinery including main engines, generators, jets, steering, stabiliser ride controls etc. Closed circuit television relays pictures from both engine spaces in the twin hulls in addition to jet spaces and hydraulic rooms. The Chief Engineer is assisted by an assistant engineer and an electrician.

The assistant engineer has a roving commission within the engine spaces and is in contact with the 'Chief' so that any problems monitored in the wheelhouse can be dealt with immediately.

A second crew takes over at night while the SeaCat is in port and supervises any repairs and carries out maintenace of various parts of the machinery. This includes topping up or changing oils and renewing or cleaning filters. Fuel and domestic fresh water are replenished every night and between sailings during the day. As weight is an important factor in the performance of a SeaCat, taking water and fuel at regular intervals keeps this to a minimum.

Conventional ships and high speed craft require a high standard of maintenance if they are to provide a reliable service. Periods in port, especially overnight, are used by the engineering department to maintain the ship and its machinery.

A survey of all engines, boilers, pumps, compressor tanks, hull, superstructures etc. is carried out by a Classification Society, such as Lloyds, and the Flag State Administration of the country where the ship is registered, every five years.

A section of these continuous surveys is carried out each year but major work such as the opening up of machinery for survey is carried out by the ship's engineers or by the shore-side workshops during the period of annual or bi-annual docking. Occasionally, time allows us to complete this work while the vessel is in service. Passenger vessels are dry-docked annually and cargo vessels every 24 - 30 months. Dry-dockings are carried out by the shipyards with our own engineers in attendance overseeing the inspection of stern tubes and variable pitch propellers while bow thrusts are checked for seal tightness.

Sea suction grids, which cover each sea water pump intakes, are cleared of marine growth which can be quite substantial now that seas, harbours and river estuaries are that much cleaner. Not many years ago, it was always said that a trip up the Manchester Ship Canal would clean all marine growth from a ship's hull and so save on dry-docking. At each fifth dry-docking, propeller tailshafts are withdrawn from the stern tubes for calibration of the shafts and stern tube bearings.

Work which cannot be attempted on passage is normally carried out at Douglas either between trips or overnight. The vessels are supported by a very competent shore staff based at Fort Street where a well-equipped and well-stocked workshop has been established for many years. Many of the staff are long-serving having completed their apprenticeship with the Company and in other cases returned to us following sailing experience with other shipping companies. This has developed a very capable and knowledgeable workforce which is able to undertake major tasks when needs arise.

A recent example of this was during the 1993 T.T. Week when the *Lady of Mann* had the misfortune to be off service for a short period. The Fort Street staff were able to effect repairs within 36 hours to the satisfaction of the surveyors and the vessel remained in service until a convenient time could be arranged to dock her. Fortunately events of this nature are very rare - the majority of the work is dealing with problems at an early stage thereby avoiding major problems.

Both the Victoria Pier and the Edward Pier linkspans, as well as car ramps and passenger gangways, also come under our wing. In addition to these, the Fort Street workshops also constructed the elevating covered walkway and gangway now at use on the Victoria Pier in Douglas and have more recently built three hydraulic operated passenger gangways for use with SeaCat operations in the Middle East.

With the reduction in the number of vessels in the present fleet, coupled with the desire to retain the expertise of the workforce, the Fort Street workshops and staff have in recent years begun to diversify. As Fort Street Marine and Industrial Services, we presently work for the hospital, milk marketing board and breweries. The general public also seek our assistance with work ranging from motor cycles to mending garden gates.

Mike Casey

Fleet List

Manxman (John Hendy)

1 MONA'S ISLE [1]　　　　Wooden paddle steamer, side lever
Built: John Wood & Co, Port Glasgow　　Engines: Robert Napier, Glasgow
Gross Tonnage: 200　　　　Speed: 8.5 knots
Overall Length: 35.36m　　　Breadth: 5.79m
Launched: 30.6.1830　　　Cost: £7,052
Disposal: sold to Robert Napier for breaking up in 1851 for £580.

2 MONA [1]　　　　Wooden paddle steamer, side lever
Built: John Wood & Co, Port Glasgow　　Engines: Robert Napier, Glasgow
Gross Tonnage: 150　　　　Speed: 9.0 knots
Overall Length: 29.87m　　　Breadth: 5.18m
Launched: 27.7.1832　　　Cost: £4,650
Disposal: sold to Liverpool Steam Tug Co. in 1841.

3 QUEEN OF THE ISLE　　　Wooden paddle steamer, side lever
Built & engined: Robert Napier, Glasgow
Gross Tonnage: 350　　　　Speed: 9.5 knots
Overall Length: 39.01m　　　Breadth: 6.55m
Launched: 3.5.1834
Disposal: sold to Napier in 1844 & converted to sail. Wrecked off Falklands.

4 KING ORRY [1]　　　　Wooden paddle steamer, side lever
Official Number: 21923　　　Call Sign: N J H M
Built: John Winram, Douglas　　Engines: Robert Napier, Glasgow
Gross Tonnage: 433　　　　Speed: 9.5 knots
Overall Length: 42.67m　　　Breadth: 7.09m
Launched: 10.2.1842　　　Cost: £10,763
Disposal: taken over by Napier in 1858 in part payment for **Douglas** [1] (£5,000 allowed). Re-sold to Greeks by Napier for trading in Eastern Mediterranean.

5 BEN-MY-CHREE [1]　　　Iron paddle steamer, side lever
Official Number: 21922　　　Call Sign: N J H L
Built and engined: Robert Napier, Glasgow　Yard No: 13
(engines ex **Queen of the Isle**)
Gross Tonnage: 458　　　　Speed: 9.5 knots
Overall Length: 50.29m　　　Breadth: 7.01m
Launched: 3.5.1845　　　Cost: £11,500
Disposal: sold in 1860 for further trading in West Africa for £1,200. Reported to be lying as a hulk in the Bonny River in 1930.

6 TYNWALD [1]　　　　Iron paddle steamer, side lever
Official Number: 21921　　　Call Sign: N J H K
Built and engined: Robert Napier, Glasgow　Yard No: 19
Gross Tonnage: 700　　　　Speed: 14 knots
Overall Length: 57.30m　　　Breadth: 8.23m
Launched: 28.4.1846　　　Cost: £21,500
Disposal: sold in 1866 for £5,000 to Caird & Co in part payment of **Tynwald** [2].

7 MONA'S QUEEN [1]　　　Iron paddle steamer, side lever
Official Number: 21930　　　Call Sign: N J H N
Built and engined: J & G Thomson, Govan　Yard No: 6
Gross Tonnage: 600　　　　Speed: 13 knots
Overall Length: 56.69m　　　Breadth: 8.23m
Launched: 27.11.1852　　　Cost: £14,000
Disposal: broken up in 1880.

8 DOUGLAS [1]　　　　Iron paddle steamer, side lever
Official Number: 20683　　　Call Sign: N C F T
Built and engined: Robert Napier, Glasgow　Yard No: 87
Gross Tonnage: 700　　　　Speed: 17 knots
Overall Length: 62.48m　　　Breadth: 7.92m
Launched: 28.4.1858　　　Cost: £22,500
Disposal: sold in 1862 for £24,000 to the Confederate Agents, Fraser Trenholm & Co. and renamed **Margaret & Jessie** as blockade runner in American Civil War. Commissioned as the **Gettysburg** in 1864. Broken up 1879 at Naples.

9 MONA'S ISLE [2]/**ELLAN VANNIN**　built as Iron paddle steamer, simple oscillating
Official Number: 27260　　　Call Sign: P Q M G
Built and engined: Tod & McGregor, Meadowside, Glasgow
Converted to twin screw steamer in 1883 by Westray, Copeland & Co., Barrow and renamed **Ellan Vannin** on 16th November 1883. 2 cylinder compound engines installed.
Gross Tonnage: 339/375 as E/V　　Speed: 12 knots/12.5 as E/V
Overall Length: 63.09m　　　Breadth: 6.71m
Launched: 10.4.1860　　　Cost: £10,673
Disposal: Foundered at Mersey Bar at 07.00 on 3rd December 1909 with loss of all on board.

10 SNAEFELL [1}　　　　Iron paddle steamer - 2 cylinder oscillating
Official Number: 45468　　　Call Sign: V D L F
Built and engined: Caird & Co., Greenock: Yard No. 105
Gross Tonnage: 700　　　　Speed: 15 knots
Overall Length: 69.68m　　　Breadth: 8.00m
Launched: 22.6.1863　　　Cost: £22,000
Disposal: sold in 1875 for £15,500 to Zeeland Steamship Co. and renamed **Stad Breda**. Broken up in 1888 at Ambacht, Holland.

11 DOUGLAS [2]　　　　Iron paddle steamer - 2 cylinder oscillating
Official Number: 45470　　　Call Sign: V D L H
Built & engined: Caird & Co., Greenock: Yard No. 112
Gross Tonnage: 709　　　　Speed 15 knots
Overall Length: 69.19m　　　Breadth: 7.98m
Launched: 11.5.1864　　　Cost: £24,869
Disposal: auctioned in January 1889 by C. W. Kellock & Co. for £1,450 for scrapping by R. P. Houston

Tynwald (2)

John Shepherd collection

Tynwald (3)

Ferry Publications Library

12 TYNWALD [2]   Iron paddle steamer - 2 cylinder
                                            oscillating
Official Number: 45474   Call Sign: H P T J
Built & engined: Caird & Co., Greenock: Yard No. 131
Gross Tonnage: 696   Speed: 15 knots
Overall Length: 73.53m   Breadth: 8.02m
Launched: 17.3.1866   Cost: £26,000
Disposal: auctioned in January 1889 by C. W. Kellock & Co. for scrapping by
George Cohen.

13 KING ORRY [2]   Iron paddle steamer - simple
                                            oscillating
Official Number: 45479   Call Sign: P K G B
Built: R. Duncan & Co., Port Glasgow: Yard No. 56
Engines: Rankin & Blackmore of Greenock.
Gross Tonnage: 809 inc. to 1104   Speed: 15 knots
Overall Length: 79.25m (as built)   Breadth: 8.94m
Launched: 27.3.1871   Cost: £26,000
Refitted by Westray, Copeland & Co., Barrow in 1888 and lengthened by
9.14m. New compound diagonal engines increased speed to 17 knots.
Disposal: broken up at Llanerch-y-Mor, Deeside in 1912.

14 BEN-MY-CHREE [2]   Iron paddle steamer, 2 cylinder
                                            oscillating
Official Number: 67288   Call Sign: P K F Q
Built & engined: Barrow Shipbuilding Co.: Yard No. 25
Refitted and re-boiled 1884 - Two additional funnels fitted
Gross Tonnage: 1030 inc. to 1192   Speed: 14 knots
Overall Length: 96.93m   Breadth: 9.45m
Launched: 6.5.1875   Cost: £38,000
Disposal: broken up in 1906 at Morecambe by T. W. Ward & Co.

Snaefell (3)

15 SNAEFELL [2]   Iron paddle steamer, simple
                                            oscillating
Official Number: 67289   Call Sign: Q W S P
Built & engined: Caird & Co., Greenock: Yard No. 202
Gross Tonnage: 849   Speed: 15 knots
Overall Length: 79.10m   Breadth: 8.91m
Launched: 27.4.1876   Cost: £28,250
Disposal: towed to Holland by tug **Ostzee** for demolition in 1904.

16 MONA [2]   Iron single screw steamer, vertical
                                            compound engines
Official Number: 76302
Built & engined: William Laird & Co., Birkenhead: Yard No. 56
Gross Tonnage: 562   Speed: 13 knots
Overall Length: 63.09m   Breadth: 7.92m
Launched: 31.5.1878   Cost: £19,500
Disposal: sank in the Formby Channel when she was run into by the Spanish
steamer **Rita** on 5th August 1883.

17 FENELLA [1]   Iron twin screw steamer, vertical
                                            compound engines
Official Number: 76303   Call Sign: J C T G
Built & engined: Barrow Shipbuilding Co. Ltd.: Yard No. 95
Gross Tonnage: 564   Speed: 14 knots
Overall Length: 63.09m   Breadth: 7.92m
Launched: 9.6.1881   Cost: £18,750
Disposal: sold for £2,290 in 1929 and broken up by John Cashmore at
Newport, Gwent.

18 MONA'S ISLE [3]   Steel paddle steamer - compound
                                            oscillating
Official Number: 76304   Call Sign: P K F C
Built & engined: Caird & Co. of Greenock: Yard No. 227
Gross Tonnage: 1564   Speed: 18 knots
Overall Length: 103.02m   Breadth: 11.58m
Launched: 16.5.1882   Cost: £58,700
Disposal: purchased by Admiralty in 1915, and broken up by T. W. Ward Ltd
at Morecambe in 1919.

19 PEVERIL [1]   Steel twin screw steamer,
                                            vertical compound engines
Official Number: 76307   Call Sign: J R Q V
Built & engined: Barrow Shipbuilding Co. Ltd: Yard No. 121
Gross Tonnage: 561   Speed: 13.5 knots
Overall Length: 65.53m   Breadth: 7.92m
Launched: 24.5.1884   Cost: £20,000
Disposal: sank off Douglas on 16th September 1899 after collision with
Monarch

20 MONA'S QUEEN [2]   Steel paddle steamer - compound
                                            oscillating
Official Number: 76308   Call Sign: K F L S
Built & engined: Barrow Shipbuilding Co. Ltd.: Yard No. 130
Gross Tonnage: 1559   Speed: 19 knots
Overall Length: 99.98m   Breadth: 11.66m
Launched: 18.4.1885   Cost: £55,000
Disposal: sold in 1929 for £5,920 for breaking up by Smith & Houston at Port
Glasgow

21 PRINCE OF WALES   Steel paddle steamer - compound
                                            diagonal
Official Number: 93381   Call Sign: P K D B
Built & engined: Fairfield Shipbuilding & Engineering Co. Ltd.: Yard No. 322
Built for IOM, Liverpool & Manchester S.S.Co. (Manx Line)
acquired by IOMSPCo.: 23.11.1888
Gross Tonnage: 1657   Speed: 20.25 knots
Overall Length: 104.09m   Breadth: 11.89m
Launched: 14.4.1887   Cost (on acquisition): £77,500
Disposal: sold to Admiralty in 1915 and name changed to **Prince Edward**. Sold
to T.C.Pas for £5,600 in 1920 and broken up Scheveningen, Holland.

22 QUEEN VICTORIA   Steel paddle steamer - compound
                                            diagonal
Official Number: 93379   Call Sign: P K C S
Built & engined: Fairfield Shipbuilding & Engineering Co. Ltd.: Yard No. 321
Built for IOM, Liverpool & Manchester S.S.Co. (Manx Line)
acquired by IOMSPCo.: 23.11.1888
Gross Tonnage: 1657   Speed: 20.25 knots
Overall Length: 104.09m   Breadth: 11.89m
Launched: 29.3.1887   Cost (on acquisition): £77,500
Disposal: sold to Admiralty 28.1.1915. Sold for breaking up at Ambacht,
Holland for £5,450 in April 1920.

Cammell Laird Archive

23 TYNWALD [3]

Steel twin screw steamer triple expansion

Official Number: 95755 | Call Sign: P K G D
Built & engined: Fairfield SB & Engr. Co. Ltd., Govan: Yard No. 356
Gross Tonnage: 937 | Speed: 18 knots:
Overall Length: 84.12m | Breadth: 10.36m
Launched: 11.5.1891 | Cost: £58,683
Disposal: Laid up 1930. Sold to R. A. Colby Cubbin in 1933 and renamed **Western Isles**. Req. by Admiralty 1939 and renamed **Eastern Isles**. Broken up La Spezia 1952.

24 EMPRESS QUEEN

Steel paddle steamer, compound diagonal

Official Number: 95759 | Call Sign: P V R M
Built & engined: Fairfield SB & Engr. Co. Ltd. Govan: Yard No. 392
Gross Tonnage: 2140 | Speed: 21.5 knots
Overall Length: 113.39m | Breadth: 13.11m
Launched: 4.3.1897 | Cost: £130,000
Disposal: Req. by Admiralty 1915. Stranded on Bembridge Ledge, IOW, 1.2.1916 and became total loss.

25 DOUGLAS [3]

Steel single screw steamer, reciprocating engines

Official Number: 94515 | Call Sign: L C S W
Built & engined: Robert Napier, Glasgow: Yard No. 416
Built as the **Dora** for the London & South Western Railway Co.: acquired 26.7.1901
Gross Tonnage: 774 | Speed: 15 knots
Overall Length: 75.89m | Breadth: 9.14m
Launched: 2.3.1889 | Cost: £13,500 (on acquisition)
Disposal: Sank in River Mersey after collision with **Artemisia** on 16.8.1923.

26 MONA [3]

Steel paddle steamer, compound diagonal

Official Number: 96575 | Call Sign: L J R V
Built & engined: Fairfield SB & Engr. Co. Ltd.: Yard No. 340
Built as **Calais-Douvres** for London, Chatham & Dover Railway Co. Sold in 1900 to Liverpool & Douglas Steamers: acquired by IOMSPCo.: July 1903.
Gross Tonnage: 1212 | Speed: 18 knots
Overall Length: 102.41m | Breadth: 10.97m
Launched: 13.4.1889 | Cost: £6,000 (on acquisition)
Disposal: Broken up at Briton Ferry by T. W. Ward Ltd. in 1909.

27 VIKING

Steel triple screw direct drive turbine steamer

Official Number: 118604 | Call Sign: H R C S: from 1934 G P M D
Built: Armstrong, Whitworth, Newcastle on Tyne: Yard No. 719
Turbines: Parsons Marine Steam Turbine Co. Ltd.
Gross Tonnage: 1957 | Speed: 22.5 knots
Overall Length: 110.03m | Breadth: 12.80m
Launched: 7.3.1905 | Cost: £83,900
Disposal: Sold to T. W. Ward Ltd. at Barrow for breaking up on 16.8.1954.

28 BEN-MY-CHREE [3]

Steel triple screw direct drive turbine steamer

Official Number: 118605 | Call Sign: H R C Q
Built & engined: Vickers, Sons & Maxim, Barrow in Furness: Yard No. 365
Gross Tonnage: 2550 | Speed: 24.5 knots
Overall Length: 118.57m | Breadth: 14.02m
Launched: 24.3.1908 | Cost: £112,100
Disposal: Sunk by gunfire at Castellorizo 11.1.1917. Raised 1920. Scrapped at Venice 1923.

29 SNAEFELL [3]

Steel twin screw steamer triple expansion

Official Number: 118606 | Call Sign: H S B Q
Built & engined: Cammell Laird & Co. Ltd., Birkenhead: Yard No. 758
Gross Tonnage: 1368 | Speed: 19 knots
Overall Length: 85.95m | Breadth: 12.60m
Launched: 12.2.1910 | Cost: £59,275
Disposal: Req. by Admiralty 1914. Torpedoed and sunk in Mediterranean 5.6.1918.

30 TYRCONNEL

Steel single screw steamer, compound engine

Official Number: 99794 | Call Sign: N D P B
Built & engined: J. Fullerton of Paisley: Yard No. 103
Acquired by Manx Steam Trading Co. in 1902. Acquired by IOMSPCo. 6.5.1911
Gross Tonnage: 274 | Speed: 9 knots
Overall Length: 41.15m | Breadth: 6.71m
Launched: 29.2.1892 | Cost: £4,875 (on acquisition)
Disposal: sold to W. J. Ireland of Liverpool January 1932. Broken up Danzig 1934.

31 THE RAMSEY

Steel twin screw steamer, reciprocating.

Official Number: 104240 | Call Sign: M N S P
Built & engined: The Naval Construction & Armaments Co., Barrow: Yard No. 243
Built as **Duke of Lancaster** for the Lancashire & Yorkshire Railway Co. Acquired by IOMSPCo.: 12.7.1912
Gross Tonnage:1621 | Speed: 17.5 knots
Overall Length: 97.54m | Breadth: 11.28m
Launched: 9.5.1895
Disposal: Requisitioned by Admiralty 1914. Sunk by German raider **Meteor** 8.8.1915.

Peel Castle

John Shepherd collection

32 PEEL CASTLE

Steel twin screw steamer, reciprocating.

Official Number: 104233 | Call Sign: J F K Q
Built & engined: William Denny & Bros., Dumbarton: Yard No. 480
Built as **Duke of York** for the Lancashire & Yorkshire Railway Co. Acquired by IOMSPCo.: 17.7.1912
Gross Tonnage: 1474 | Speed: 17.5 knots
Overall Length: 97.84m | Breadth: 11.28m
Launched: 28.2.1894
Disposal: broken up by Arnott Young at Dalmuir, Clyde, February 1939.

33 KING ORRY [3]

Steel twin screw steamer, geared turbines

Official Number: 118608 | Call Sign: J F P C: from 1934 G P M F
Built & engined: Cammell Laird & Co. Ltd., Birkenhead: Yard No. 789
Gross Tonnage: 1877 | Speed: 20.75 knots
Overall Length: 95.40m | Breadth: 13.11m
Launched: 11.3.1913 | Cost: £96,000
Disposal: Bombed and sunk in the evacuation of Dunkirk, 30.5.1940.

34 MONA [4]

Official Number: 124188

Built & engined: Fairfield SB & Engr. Co. Ltd., Govan: Yard No. 451
Built as **Hazel** for the Laird Line.

Gross Tonnage: 1219
Overall Length: 81.69m
Launched: 13.4.1907
Disposal: sold to E. G. Rees of Llanelli for breaking up, December 1938.

Steel twin screw steamer, triple expansion

Call Sign: H K T G: from 1934 G F B Y

Acquired by IOMSPCo.: 21.5.1919
Speed: 16 knots
Breadth: 10.97m
Cost: £65,000 (on acquisition)

Manxman (1)

35 MANXMAN [1]

Official Number: 118603

Built & engined: Vickers, Sons & Maxim, Barrow: Yard No. 315
Built as **Manxman** for Midland Railway Co.: Acquired by IOMSPCo: March 1920

Gross Tonnage: 2030
Overall Length: 103.94m
Launched: 15.6.1904
Disposal: Requisitioned by Admiralty 1939. Broken up by T. W. Ward at Preston 1949.

Steel triple screw steamer, direct drive turbines

Call Sign: H M R S: from 1934 G F P S

Speed: 22 knots
Breadth: 13.11m

36 MONA'S ISLE [4]

Official Number: 120522

Built & engined: William Denny & Bros., Dumbarton: Yard No. 751
Built as **Onward** for South Eastern & Chatham Railway Co.
Acquired by IOMSPCo.: May 1920
Gross Tonnage: 1691
Overall Length: 96.93m
Launched: 11.3.1905
Disposal: Sold for breaking up in October 1948 and towed to Milford Haven.

Steel triple screw steamer, direct drive turbines

Call Sign: H C M F: from 1934 G F P M

Name changed: 27.8.1920
Speed: 21 knots
Breadth: 12.19m

37 SNAEFELL [4]

Official Number: 121331

Built & engined: Fairfield SB & Engr. Co. Ltd., Govan: Yard No. 444
Built as **Viper** for G. & J. Burns.

name changed: 22.7.1920
Gross Tonnage: 1713
Overall Length: 99.21m
Launched: 10.3.1906
Disposal: sold to Smith & Houston, Port Glasgow 1945, scrapped 1948.

Steel triple screw steamer, direct drive turbines

Call Sign: H G F M: from 1934 G P M K

Acquired by IOMSPCo.: 22.3.1920

Speed: 21 knots
Breadth: 12.04m
Cost: £60,000 (on acquisition)

38 CUSHAG

Official Number: 124673
Built & engined: George Brown & Co., Greenock: Yard No. 50
Built as **Ardnagrena** for J. Waterson, Co. Antrim: sold in 1914 to Humber Steam Coasters.
Acquired by IOMSPCo.: May 1920
Gross Tonnage: 223
Overall Length: 39.62m
Launched: 12.8.1908
Disposal: Sold 26.1.1943 to T. Dougal and registered Stornoway: broken up Grangemouth July 1957.

Steel single screw steamer, compound engines

Call Sign: M D Y P

Name changed: 27.8.1920
Speed: 10 knots
Breadth: 6.71m
Cost: £22,000 (on acquisition)

39 MANX MAID [1]

Official Number: 131763

Built & engined: Cammell Laird & Co. Ltd., Birkenhead: Yard No. 761
Built as **Caesarea** for London & South Western Railway Co.
Acquired by IOMSPCo.: 27.11.1923.
Gross Tonnage: 1504
Overall Length: 90.83m
Launched: 26.5.1910
Disposal: Broken up at Barrow in 1950 by T. W. Ward & Co. Ltd.

Steel triple screw steamer, direct drive turbines

Call Sign: H R Q M: from 1934 G K M F

Speed: 20 knots
Breadth: 11.89m
Cost: £38,500 (inc. complete refit)

Ben-my-Chree (4)

40 BEN-MY-CHREE [4]

Official Number: 145304

Built & engined: Cammell Laird & Co. Ltd., Birkenhead: Yard No. 926
Gross Tonnage: 2586
Overall Length: 111.56m
Launched: 5.4.1927
Maiden Voyage: 29.6.1927
Disposal: Left Birkenhead under tow of tug **Fairplay XI** on 18.12.1965 for shipbreakers at Ghent.

Steel twin screw steamer, geared turbines

Call Sign: L C F G: from 1934 G N D B

Speed: 22.5 knots
Breadth: 14.02m
Cost: £200,000
Final Voyage: 13.9.1965

41 VICTORIA

Official Number: 123811

Built & engined: William Denny & Bros., Dumbarton: Yard No. 789
Built as **Victoria** for South Eastern & Chatham Railway Co.
Acquired by IOMSPCo.: 1928
Gross Tonnage: 1641
Overall Length: 98.15m
Launched: 27.2.1907
Disposal: Last voyage: 18.8.1956. Towed from Birkenhead to Barrow 25.1.1957 and broken up by T. W. Ward & Co. Ltd.

Steel triple screw steamer, direct drive turbines

Call Sign: H K N R: from 1934 G N T F

Speed: 21 knots
Breadth: 12.19m
Cost: £25,000 (on acquisition)

John Shepherd collection

Raymond Brandreth collection

Conister (1)

42 RAMSEY TOWN Steel twin screw steamer, triple expansion reciprocating
Official Number: 116015 Call Sign: H M S B
Built & engined: John Brown & Co. Ltd., Clydebank: Yard No. 363
Built as **Antrim** for the Midland Railway Co.
Acquired by IOMSPCo.: 11.5.1928
Gross Tonnage: 1954 Speed: 20 knots
Overall Length: 103.63m Breadth: 12.80m
Launched: 22.4.1904 Cost: £14,612 (on acquisition)
Disposal: Broken up at Preston in October 1936 by T. W. Ward & Co. Ltd.

43 RUSHEN CASTLE Steel twin screw steamer, triple expansion reciprocating
Official Number: 109661 Call Sign: Q F W M: from 1934 G F R X
Built & engined: Vickers, Sons & Maxim Ltd., Barrow: Yard No. 264
Built as **Duke of Cornwall** for the Lancashire & Yorkshire and London & North Western Railway Companies' Joint Service
Acquired by IOMSPCo.: 11.5.1928
Gross Tonnage: 1724 Speed: 17.5 knots
Overall Length: 97.84m Breadth: 11.28m
Launched: 23.4.1898 Cost: £29,254 (on acquisition)
Disposal: Last voyage: 14.9.1946. Towed from Douglas to Ghent on 9.1.1947 by tug **Ganges** for demolition.

44 PEVERIL [2] Steel single screw steamer, triple expansion
Official Number: 145306 Call Sign: M B F C
Built & engined: Cammell Laird & Co. Ltd., Birkenhead: Yard No. 957
Gross Tonnage: 798 Speed: 12 knots
Overall Length: 64.92m Breadth: 10.52m
Launched: 25.4.1929 Cost: £42,600
Disposal: Broken up at Glasson Dock, May 1964.

45 LADY OF MANN [1] Steel twin screw steamer, geared turbines
Official Number: 145307 Call Sign: LG C Q: from 1934 G M K Z
Built & engined: Vickers Armstrong Ltd., Barrow: Yard No. 660
Gross Tonnage: 3104 Speed: 22.5 knots
Overall length: 113.08m Breadth: 15.30m
Launched: 4.3.1930 Cost: £249,073
Maiden Voyage: 28.6.1930 Final Voyage: 17.8.1971
Disposal: Left Barrow 29.12.1971 under tow of tug **Wrestler**, for breaking up by Arnott Young at Dalmuir, arriving 31.12.1971.

46 CONISTER [1] Steel single screw steamer, triple expansion reciprocating
Official Number: 145470 Call Sign: K L F W: from 1934 M K W Q
Built & engined: Goole Shipbuilding Co. Ltd., Goole: Yard No. 4
Built as **Abington** for G. T. Gillie & Blair, Newcastle: Acquired by IOMSPCo.: 8.1.1932
Gross Tonnage: 411 Speed: 10 knots
Overall Length: 44.20m Breadth: 7.31m
Launched: 13.9.1921 Cost: £5,500 (on acquisition)
Disposal: Left Douglas under tow of tug **Campaigner** for breaking up by Arnott Young, Dalmuir on 26.1.1965.

47 MONA'S QUEEN [3] Steel twin screw steamer, geared turbines
Official Number: 145308 Call Sign: G W S G
Built & engined: Cammell Laird & Co. Ltd., Birkenhead: Yard No. 998
Gross Tonnage: 2756 Speed: 21.5 knots
Overall Length: 106.68m Breadth: 14.63m
Launched: 12.4.1934 Cost: £201,250
Disposal: Mined and sunk at Dunkirk: 29.5.1940

48 FENELLA [2] Steel twin screw steamer, geared turbines
Official Number: 145310 Call Sign: G Z N Y
Built & engined: Vickers Armstrong Ltd., Barrow: Yard No. 718
Gross Tonnage: 2376 Speed: 21 knots
Overall Length: 95.86m Breadth: 14.02m
Launched: 16.12.1936 Cost: £203,550
Disposal: Sunk by air attack at Dunkirk: 29.5.1940

49 TYNWALD [4] Steel twin screw steamer, geared turbines
Official Number: 165281 Call Sign: G Z R L
Built & engined: Vickers Armstrong Ltd., Barrow: Yard No. 717
Gross Tonnage: 2376 Speed: 21.5 knots
Overall Length: 95.86m Breadth: 14.02m
Launched: 16.12.1936 Cost: £203,550
Disposal: Torpedoed and sunk at Bougie, Algeria, 12.11.1942

50 KING ORRY [4] Steel twin screw steamer, geared turbines
Official Number: 165282 Call Sign: G M J M
Built & engined: Cammell Laird & Co. Ltd., Birkenhead: Yard No. 1169
Gross Tonnage: 2485 Speed: 21.5 knots
Overall Length: 105.19m Breadth: 14.38m
Launched: 22.11.1945 Cost: £402,095
Maiden Voyage: 18.1.1946 Final Voyage: 31.8.1975
Disposal: Towed to Glasson Dock by tug **Sea Bristolian** 5.11.1975. Towed to Kent and broken up Strood (arrived 11.1.1978), late 1979.

51 MONA'S QUEEN [4] Steel twin screw steamer, geared turbines
Official Number: 165283 Call Sign: G M J R
Built & engined: Cammell Laird & Co. Ltd., Birkenhead: Yard No. 1170
Gross Tonnage: 2485 Speed: 21.5 knots
Overall Length: 105.16m Breadth: 14.38m
Launched: 5.2.1946 Cost: £411,241
Maiden Voyage: 26.6.1946 Final Voyage: 16.9.1961
Disposal: Left Barrow under own steam 12.11.1962 renamed **Barrow Queen** bound for Piraeus for further service as **Fiesta** for Chandris Lines. Broken up Perama 9.1981.

52 TYNWALD [5] — Steel twin screw steamer, geared turbines

Official Number: 165284 — Call Sign: G J V X
Built & engined: Cammell Laird & Co. Ltd., Birkenhead: Yard No. 1184
Gross Tonnage: 2487 — Speed: 21.5 knots
Overall Length: 105.12m — Breadth: 14.38m
Launched: 24.3.1947 — Cost: £461,859
Maiden Voyage: 31.7.1947 — Final Voyage: 26.8.1974
Disposal: Sold to John Cashmore Ltd., Newport, Gwent for breaking up in November 1974, but re-sold and towed to Spanish shipbreakers at Aviles by tug **Sea Bristolian** on 3.2.1975

53 SNAEFELL [5] — Steel twin screw steamer, geared turbines

Official Number: 165287 — Call Sign: M A V K
Built & engined: Cammell Laird & Co. Ltd., Birkenhead: Yard No. 1192.
Gross Tonnage: 2489 — Speed: 21.5 knots
Overall Length: 105.11m — Breadth: 14.38m
Launched: 11.3.1948 — Cost: £504,448
Maiden Voyage: 24.7.1948 — Final Voyage: 29.8.1977
Disposal: Sold to Rochdale Metal Recovery Company and towed by tug **George V** to Blyth, Northumberland on 24.8.1978. Arrived 8.9.1978 and broken up by H. Kitson, Vickers & Co.

54 MONA'S ISLE [5] — Steel twin screw steamer, geared turbines

Official Number: 165288 — Call Sign: G C X Y
Built & engined: Cammell Laird & Co. Ltd., Birkenhead: Yard No. 1209
Gross Tonnage: 2491 — Speed: 21.5 knots
Overall Length: 105.16m — Breadth: 14.38m
Launched: 12.10.1950 — Cost: £570,000
Maiden Voyage: 22.3.1951 — Final Voyage: 27.8.1980
Disposal: Left Birkenhead under tow of tug **Afon Wen** on 30.10.1980 for Dutch shipbreakers Sloop-Berginsbedrijf van de Marec.

55 FENELLA [3] — Steel single screw diesel motorship
Official Number: 165289 — Call Sign: M L F M
Built & engined: Ailsa Shipbuilding Co. Ltd., Troon: Yard No. 472
Gross Tonnage: 1019 — Speed: 12.5 knots
Overall Length: 64.01m — Breadth: 11.28m
Launched: 6.8.1951 — Cost: £163,783
Disposal: Sold to Cypriot Juliet Shipping Co. and left Birkenhead on 9.2.1973 as the **Vasso M** for further trading. Caught fire and sank in the eastern Mediterranean, May 1978.

Manxman (2)

Captain Vernon Kinley

56 MANXMAN [2] — Steel twin screw steamer, geared turbines

Official Number: 186349 — Call Sign: M T Q C
Built & engined: Cammell Laird & Co. Ltd., Birkenhead: Yard No. 1259
Gross Tonnage: 2495 — Speed: 21.5 knots
Overall Length: 105.11m — Breadth: 15.24m
Launched: 8.2.1955 — Cost: £847,000
Maiden Voyage: 21.5.1955 — Final Voyage: 4.9.1982
Disposal: Sold to Marda (Squash) Ltd. and sailed under own steam to Preston

Dock on 3.10.1982, carrying 1,000 passengers. Left Preston under tow of **Afon Las** on 5.11.1990, arriving Liverpool 6.11.90. Left Liverpool 16.4.1994 under tow of **Freebooter** bound for Hull for use as nightclub.

Manx Maid (2)

John Hendy

57 MANX MAID [2] — Steel twin screw steamer, geared turbines

Official Number: 186352 — Call Sign: G H X Y
Built & engined: Cammell Laird & Co. Ltd., Birkenhead: Yard No. 1303
Gross Tonnage: 2724 — Speed: 21.5 knots
Overall Length: 104.83m — Breadth: 16.16m
Launched: 23.1.1962 — Cost: £1,087,000
Maiden Voyage: 23.5.1962 — Final Voyage: 9.9.1984
Disposal: Left Birkenhead under tow for Bristol 10.4.1985. Left Avonmouth 8.2.1986 under tow of tug **Indomitable** for Garston, Merseyside, for breaking up.

58 PEVERIL [3] — Steel single screw diesel motorship
Official Number: 186353 — Call Sign: G M O G
Built & engined: Ailsa Shipbuiding Co. Ltd., Troon: Yard No. 516
Converted to a Cellular Container Ship 1972 - Capacity 56 TEU
Gross Tonnage: 1048 — Speed: 12 knots
Overall Length: 62.48m — Breadth: 11.89m
Launched: 6.12.1963 — Cost: £279,921
Disposal: Final Voyage 19.6.1981. Sold for further trading as **Nadalena H.**

59 RAMSEY — Steel single screw diesel motorship
Official Number: 186354 — Call Sign: G P J H
Built & engined: Ailsa Shipbuilding Co. Ltd., Troon: Yard No. 519
Gross Tonnage: 446 — Speed: 10 knots
Overall Length: 45.42m — Breadth: 8.53m
Launched: 6.11.1964 — Cost: £158,647
Disposal: Sold to R. Lapthorn & Co. of Rochester for further trading and re-named **Hoofort**. Left Birkenhead 9.1.1974. Re-sold in 1982 for further trading in the Cape Verde Islands and re-named **Boa Entrado**.

60 BEN-MY-CHREE [5} — Steel twin screw steamer, geared turbines

Official Number: 186355 — Call Sign: G R X Y
Built & engined: Cammell Laird & Co. Ltd., Birkenhead: Yard No. 1320
Gross Tonnage: 2762 — Speed: 21.5 knots
Overall Length: 104.83m — Breadth: 16.13m
Launched: 10.12.1965 — Cost: £1,400,000
Maiden Voyage: 12.5.1966 — Final Voyage: 19.9.1984
Disposal: Sold to New England Development Co. of Cincinnati for use as restaurant ship at Jacksonville, Florida, USA. Chartered back to IOMSPCo. from 25.5.1985 until 10.6.1985. Re-sold to shipbreakers at Santander, Spain. Left Birkenhead under tow of tug **Hollygarth** on 16.8.1989.

Above: The **Ben-my-Chree** (4) of 1927. *(W.S.Basnett)*
Below:- The **Lady of Mann** (1) was the centenary steamer. *(W.S.Basnett)*

61 MONA'S QUEEN [5] — Steel twin screw 10 Cyl. Pielstick diesel motorship.

Official Number: 307621 — Call Sign: G P O W
Built: Ailsa Shipbuilding Co. Ltd., Troon: Yard No. 533
Gross Tonnage: 2998 — Speed: 21 knots
Length overall: 104.45m — Breadth: 16.74m
Launched: 22.12.1972 — Cost: £2,100,000
Disposal: Final Voyage 3.9.1990. Laid up Vittoria Dock, Birkenhead. Future uncertain.

62 CONISTER [2] — Steel single screw Sulzer motorship
Official Number: 187114 — Call Sign: G T V B
Built: 1955: George Brown & Co. Ltd., Greenock: Yard No. 262
Built as **Brentfield** for Zillah Shipping Co.: In 1959 became **Spaniel** of Coast Lines' Group. Acquired by IOMSPCo.: November 1973 (on charter July/November 1973)
Gross Tonnage: 891 — Speed: 11 knots
Length: 68.28m — Breadth: 11.58m
Capacity 46 TEU — Cost: £96,711 (on acquisition)
Disposal: Final voyage: 16.6.1981. Sold for breaking up at Aviles, Spain in November 1981.

63 LADY OF MANN [2] — Steel twin screw 12 Cyl. Pielstick diesel motorship
Official Number: 359761 — Call Sign: G V E Q
Built: Ailsa Shipbuilding Co. Ltd., Troon: Yard No. 547
Gross Tonnage: 2990 (inc. to 3083 in 1989) — Speed: 22 knots
Length: 104.43m — Breadth: 16.74m
Launched: 4.12.1975 — Cost: £3,800,000
Disposal: Final voyage: 27.6.1994. Laid up Vittoria Dock, Birkenhead. Future uncertain.

64 PEVERIL [4] — Steel twin screw Pielstick diesel motorship
Official Number: 362507 — Call Sign: G U Q N
Built: Kristiansands Mek Ver A/S, Norway: Yard No. 216
Built 1971 as **Holmia** for Silja Line; in 1973 became **ASD Meteor** of International Ship Chartering of Singapore and chartered to Sealink and renamed **Penda** until 1980. Name changed to **NF Jaguar** in P&O Group, Normandy Ferries. In 1981 **NF Jaguar** bareboat chartered by IOMSPCo. In November 1982 James Fisher of Barrow purchased **NF Jaguar** and chartered her to IOMSPCo. on long term bareboat basis on agreed demise charter terms over 10 years. Name changed to **Peveril** [4].
Gross Tonnage: 1975 — Speed: 14 knots
Length: 106.28m — Breadth: 16.03m
Purchased outright by IOMSPCo. with a 'one-off' payment to James Fisher, May 1993. Vessel still in service.

Mona's Isle

Captain Vernon Kinley

65 MONA'S ISLE [6] — Steel twin screw M.A.N. diesel motorship.
Official Number: 307718 — Call Sign: G S N A
Built: NV Werf Gusto, Schiedam, Holland
Built as **Free Enterprise III** for Townsend Car Ferries, from 1968 Townsend-Thoresen. Sold to Mira Shipping Line in July 1984 and renamed **Tamira**. Acquired by IOMSPCo. 26.10.1984 at Valletta, Malta and renamed **Mona's Isle**
Gross Tonnage: 4657 — Speed: 21 knots, maximum
Length overall: 117.51m — Breadth: 19.08m
Launched: 14.5.1966 — Cost: £600,000 (on acquisition by IOMSPCo.)
Maiden Voyage for IOMSPCo.: 5.4.1985 — Final Voyage: 5.10.1985
Disposal: sold to Saudi Arabian owners for £710,500 and renamed **Al Fahad**. Left Birkenhead 7.4.1986 for further service in Red Sea.

66 MANX VIKING — Steel twin screw Pielstick diesel motorship
Official Number: 359765 — Call Sign: G Z I A
Built: S.A. Juliana Const. Gijonesa, Gijon, Spain: Yard No. 243
Built as **Monte Castillo** for Naveria Aznar, Bilbao, Spain in 1976.
Sold to Manx Line and renamed **Manx Viking** in March 1978. (Sealink/Manx Line from 20.10.1978. Manx Line merged with IOMSPCo. 1.4.1985 and **Manx Viking** taken on bareboat charter @ £1,500/day winter, £2,500/day summer.
Gross Tonnage: 3589 — Speed: 17 knots
Length: 100.50m — Breadth: 16.76m
Disposal: Final voyage: 29.9.1986. Sold to Norwegian owners in February 1987 and renamed **Skudenes**.
In April 1989 re-sold for service on the Canadian Great Lakes and renamed **Nindawayma** on the Tobermory/South Baymouth route across Georgian Bay.

67 TYNWALD [6] — Steel twin screw Pielstick diesel motorship
Official Number: 168903 — Call Sign: G X S U
Built: Hawthorn Leslie, Hebburn on Tyne: Yard No. 765
Built as **Antrim Princess** for Caledonian Steam Packet (Irish Services) Ltd. Chartered to IOMSPCo. from 5.10.1985, first voyage 6.10.1985
Gross Tonnage: 3762 — Speed: 19.5 knots
Length overall: 112.63m — Breadth: 17.40m
Launched: 24.4.1967
Disposal: Final voyage: 19.2.1990. Laid up River Fal. Sold to Agostino Lauro of Naples and renamed **Lauro Express**. Left Falmouth 25.5.1990.

Tynwald (6)

Miles Cowsill

68 KING ORRY [5] — Steel twin screw Pielstick diesel motorship

Call Sign: F N K C
Built: Cantieri Navali di Pietra Ligure, Italy: Yard No. 12
Built as **Saint Eloi**, renamed **Channel Entente** in May 1989
Gross Tonnage: 4649 — Speed: 19 knots
Length overall: 114.59m — Breadth: 18.62m
Launched: 26.2.1972 — Cost: £4.15 million (on acquisition by IOMSPCo.)
Acquired by IOMSPCo. 14.2.1990 — First voyage: 19.2.1990 as **Channel Entente**
Renamed **King Orry** 8.12.1990. Still in service.

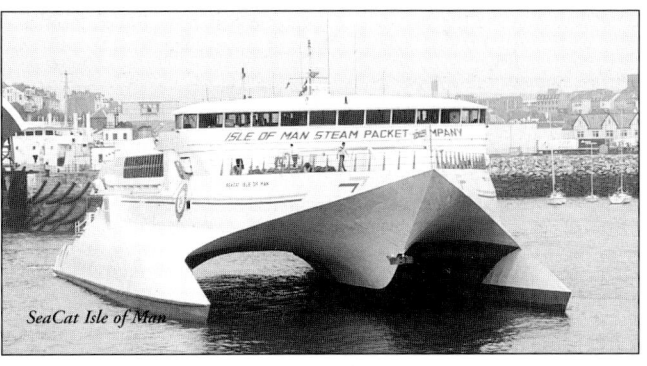

Belard

Captain Vernon Kinley

69 BELARD — Steel single screw MaK diesel motorship

Official Number: 706568
Built 1979 by Frederikshavn Vaerft A/S, Frederikshavn: Yard No. 380
Gross Tonnage: 1599 — Speed: 15 knots
Length overall: 105.62m — Breadth: 18.83m
Capacity: 51 trailers
Chartered by Mannin Line from Pandoro Ltd.: first voyage 23.11.1993.
Purchased from Pandoro Ltd.: 15.8.1994. Cost £3.2 million.

SeaCat Isle of Man

Richard Kirkman

70 SEACAT ISLE OF MAN — Aluminium hulled fast craft catamaran.

Built: International Catamarans Pty. Ltd., Hobart, Tasmania
Built 1991 as **Hoverspeed France**, chartered to Mediterranean operators as **Sardegna Express**; returned to UK and renamed **SeaCat Boulogne**.
Propulsion: 4 x 16 cylinder medium speed Ruston 16RK 270 marine diesel engines linked directly to 4 x Riva Lips BV waterjets.
Length overall: 73.6m — Breadth: 26.3m
Displacement tonnage: approx 700 tonnes unloaded
Speed: 37 knots (cruising), 42 knots maximum
On charter to IOMSPCo. from Sea Containers from 20.6.1994.
First voyage: Douglas to Fleetwood: 28.6.1994.
Final seasonal crossing: Douglas to Liverpool 26.9.1994.

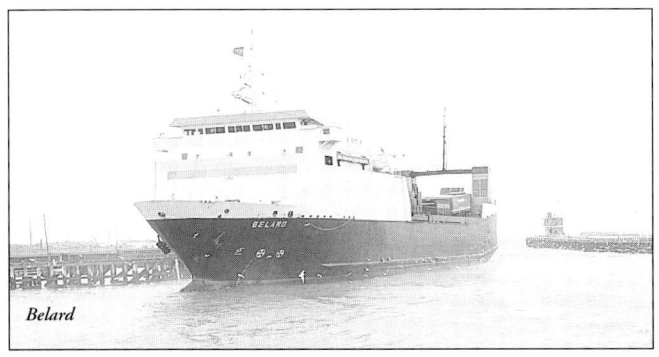

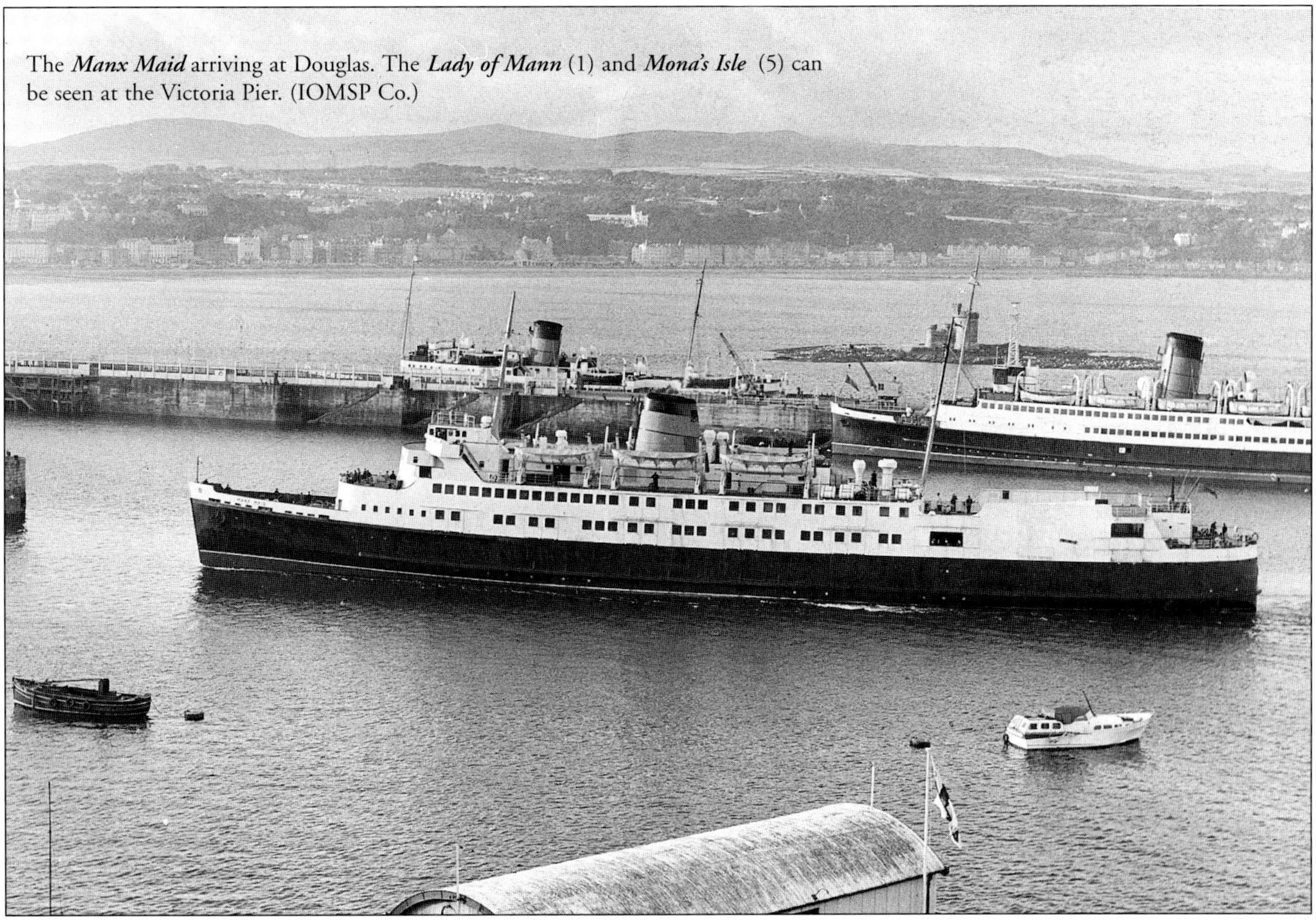

The *Manx Maid* arriving at Douglas. The *Lady of Mann* (1) and *Mona's Isle* (5) can be seen at the Victoria Pier. (IOMSP Co.)

OPPOSITION COMPANIES

Isle of Man, Liverpool & Manchester Steamship Company Limited (Manx Line)

1887/1888   Route: Liverpool and Douglas

Paddle Steamers *Queen Victoria* and *Prince of Wales* - See Fleet List Nos 21 and 22.
Taken over by IOMSPCo on 23rd November 1888.

New Isle of Man Steam Navigation Company (Lancashire Line)

1887/May 1888   Route: Liverpool and Douglas

Lancashire Witch: Steel screw steamer: 762 gross tons, 68.58m length, 9.20m breadth built in 1887 by J L Thompson & Sons, Sunderland for The New Isle of Man Steam Navigation Company Limited. Vessel sold by order of the mortgagees in May 1888.

Mutual Line of Manx Steamers

May/July 1895   Route: Liverpool and Douglas

Lady Tyler: Iron paddle steamer: 1010 gross tons, 79.55m length, 9.20m breadth, built in 1880 by T & W Smith, North Shields, for The Great Eastern Railway Company.

1897: Messrs H & C McIver advertised a new Liverpool and Douglas service as starting at Easter. To prevent the service starting the Isle of Man Steam Packet Company purchased the two steamers intended for the service, and immediately disposed of them for scrap.

Munster: Iron paddle steamer: 1750 gross tons, 99.37m, 10.73m breadth built in 1860 by J Laird of Birkenhead for City of Dublin Steam Packet Company.

Leinster: Iron paddle steamer: 1716 gross tons, 104.55m length, 10.67m breadth built in 1860 by J Samuda, London, for City of Dublin Steam Packet Company.

Liverpool and North Wales Steamship Company Limited

1896/1961   Route: Llandudno and Douglas

St.Elvies (1896/1930) Steel paddle steamer: 567 gross tons, 73.30m length, 8.61m breadth, built in 1896 by Fairfield S B & Engr Company Limited, Govan.
St Seiriol (1931/1961) Steel twin screw turbine steamer: 1586 gross tons, 82.20m length, 11.31m breadth built in 1931 by Fairfield S B & Engr Company Limited, Govan. The *St.Seiriol* was sold for scrap at the end of the 1961 season, and the Isle of Man Steam Packet Company took over the Llandudno and Douglas route from 1962/1982.

Liverpool and Douglas Steamers

1899/1902   Route: Liverpool and Douglas

Ireland: Steel paddle steamer: 2095 gross tons, 111.63m length, 11.66m breadth built 1885 by Laird Bros at Birkenhead for City of Dublin Steam Packet Company.

Lily: Steel paddle steamer: 1175 gross tons, 91.44m length, 10.09m breadth built 1880 by Laird Bros at Birkenhead for London & North Western Railway Company.

Violet: Steel paddle steamer: 1175 gross tons, 91.44m length, 10.09m breadth built 1880 by Laird Bros at Birkenhead for London & North Western Railway Company.

Brittany: Iron paddle steamer: 678 gross tons, 71.93m length, 7.70m breadth built 1864 by J Ash & Company, London, for London & South Western Railway Company

Normandy: Steel paddle steamer: 605 gross tons, 70.41m length, 8.38m breadth built 1882 by J Elder & Company, Glasgow for London, Brighton & South Coast Railway Company.

Calais-Douvres: Steel paddle steamer: 1212 gross tons, 102.41m length, 10.97m breadth built 1889 by Fairfield S B & Engr Company Limited for London, Chatham & Dover Railway Company. Acquired by IOMSPCo in July 1903 - see Fleet List No 26. Liverpool & Douglas Steamers went into liquidation in December 1902.

Norwest Hovercraft Limited

April/September 1969   Route: Fleetwood & Douglas

Stella Marina: steel twin screw motor vessel: 1339 gross tons, 77.57m length,12.04m breadth built 1965 by Rolandwerft GmbH, Bremen, for M A Eilertsen, Fredrikstad

---

Norwest Shipping Limited

June/September 1970:   Route: Fleetwood & Douglas

Norwest Laird: steel twin screw motor vessel 577 gross tons, 58.06m length, 9.77m breadth built 1939 by Wm Denny & Bros, Dumbarton as *Lochiel* for David MacBrayne Limited.

Manx Line Limited (March/October 1978)
Sealink/Manx Line Limited (October 1978/March 1985)

Route: Heysham and Douglas

Merged with Isle of Man Steam Packet Company Limited on 1st April 1985.

Manx Viking: see Fleet List No 66

The *Manx Maid* leaving the Mersey in the late sixties. *(IOMSP Co)*

THE ISLE OF MAN STEAM PACKET COMPANY LIMITED
Sailing Arrangements – Monday, 7th August to Sunday, 13th August, 1939.

	Mon, 7th August	Tues, 8th August	Wed, 9th August	Thurs, 10th August	Fri, 11th August	Sat, 12th August	Sun, 13th August
Lady of Mann	F. to D. 1030 / D. to L. 2355 / & Oil	L. to D. 1030 / D. to F. 1800	F. to D. 1030 – 1st / D. to F. 1800 – 1st	F. to D. 1030 / D. to L. 1600 / & Oil	L. to D. 1030 / D. to F. 1600	F. to D. 0130 – 1st / D. to F. 0630 / F. to D. 1030 – 1st / D. to F. 1600	F. to D. 1045 / D. to F. 1730
Ben-My-Chree	L. to D. 0100 / D. to L. 1600	L. to D. 1530	D. to L. 2355	L. to D 1030 / D. to F. 1800	F. to D. 1030 / D. to L. 1600 / L. to D. pm	D. to L. 0530 / L. to D. 1000 / D. to L. 1500	L. to D. 1045 / D. to L. 1730
Mona's Queen	Dublin to D. 0830 / D. to Dublin 2355	Dublin to D. am / D. to L. 1600 / & Oil	L. to D. 1030	D. to Dublin 0830 / Dublin to D. 1800	D. to Ard. 1000 & Oil / Ard. to D. 2300 / not Ram. to or from	D. to L. 0630 / L. to D. 1030 / D. to L. 1645 & Oil	L. to D. 0145
Tynwald	L. to D. 0030 & Oil / L to D. 1030 / D. to Dublin 1700 / Dublin to D. pm	D. to Dublin 0830 / Dublin to D. 1730	D. to Bel. 0830 / Bel. to D. 1700 / call Ram. to & from	D. to L. 0900 / fill up oil / L. to D. 1530	D. to Dublin 0830 / Dublin to D. 1730 / D. to L. 2355	L. to D. 0600 / D. to L. 0900 & Oil / L. to D. 1730	Army / D. to Hey 0900 / Hey to D. 1400
Fenella	D. to Ard. 2355 / not Ram. Oil at Ard / Ard. to D. 1200 / (call Ramsey)	D. to Llan. 0930 / Llan. to D. 1800	D. to F. 1600 / F. to Hey. 2100 / Hey. to D. pm	Round the Island 1430 / call Ramsey 1515	D. to L. 0900 / L. to D. 1530	D. to F. 0730 / F. to D. 1030 – 2nd / D. to L. 1600	
Manxman	D. to Bel. 0830 / Bel. to D. 1700 / call Ram to & from	D. to L. 0900			D. to L. 0050	D. to L. 0730 / L. to D. 1130 / D. to L. 1730	
Viking	F. to D. 1600 / & coal - 100 tons	F. to D. 1030	D. to L. 1600	Fill up coal	L. to F. am / & coal (30 tons)	F. to D. 0130 – 2nd / D. to L. 0800 / L. to D. 1400 / D. to L. 2355 – 1st	
King Orry	D. to L. 0900 & Oil / L. to D. 1530	D. to Ard. 0900 / Call Ramsey / fill up oil	Ard. to D. 1200		D. to Bel. 0930 / Bel. to D. 1700 / call Ram. to & from	D. to L. 0830 / L. to D. 1530 / D. to L. 2355 – 2nd	
Snaefell	Hey. to D. 1000 / D. to Hey. 1600	Hey. to D. 1000 / D. to Hey. 1600	Hey. to D. 1000 / D. to Hey. 1600	Hey. to D. 1000 / D. to Hey. 1600	Hey. to D. 1000 / D. to Hey. 1600	Hey. to D. 0100 / D. to Hey. 0645 / Hey. to D. 1000 / D. to H. 1600	
Victoria	Workington to D. 0515 / call Ramsey / D. to Workington 2355 / Not to call Ramsey	Workington to D. am	D. to L. 0900 & Oil / L. to D. 1530	coal at F. / F. to D. / D. to F.	D. to Ard. 0900 / call Ramsey / Ard. to D. 2330 / not to call Ramsey	D. to F. 0800 / F. to D. 1100	
Mona's Isle	D. to L. 1730 / fill up coal	L. to D. am / D. to F. 1600 / F. to Hey. 2100 / Hey. to F: pm & coal	'If Required' / F. to D. 1030 - 2nd / D. to F. 1800 - 2nd	F. to D. am / D. to F. 1600	Fill up coal	F. to D. 0130 – 3rd / D. to F. 0830 / F. to D. 1530	
Manx Maid	Barrow to D. 0200 / D. to Barrow 2355	Barrow to L. am			L. to Ramsey 1345 / Ram. to D. pm	D. to Hey. 0800 / Hey. to D. 1030	
Rushen Castle				D. to Ramsey pm	Ram. to L. 0830 / L. to D. 2355 - 2nd	D. to Hey. 0900 & Coal / Hey. to D. 1530	
Peveril	D. to L. 1700 & dock		L. to D. 1700 ex dock	D. to L. 1800 & dock	1900 from / D. to L. dock	D. to L. 2300 & dock	
Conister		L. to Ramsey 1700	Ramsey to L. 1700	L. to D. 1800	D. to L. 2100	L. to D. 2000	
Cushag	Peel to L. 1600	L. to D. 1700	D. to L. 1700	L. to C'town 1800	C'town to PSM 2000	PSM to Peel 2100	